T H E

ARMCHAIR MECHANIC

A Non-Mechanic's Guide to Understanding Your Car and Getting Good Repairs

By JACK GILLIS & TOM KELLY

PERENNIAL LIBRARY

Harper & Row Publishers, New York
Cambridge, Philadelphia, San Francisco, Washington
London, Mexico City, São Paulo, Singapore, Sydney

Library of Congress Cataloging-in-Publication Data

Gillis, Jack.
  The armchair mechanic.

  Includes index.
  1. Automobiles—Maintenance and repair—Amateurs' manuals.   I. Kelly, Tom,
1922–   II. Title.
TL 152.G519   1988   629.28'722   87-45618
ISBN 0-06-096250-X (pbk.)

88 89 90 91 92   RRD   10 9 8 7 6 5 4 3 2 1

CONTENTS

Acknowledgements   6

Introduction   7

Finding A Good Mechanic   11
  Choosing a Repair Shop   13
  Certification: What Is It?   15
  For Good Repairs, Find a Good Diagnostician   17
  How Much Should It Cost?   19
  The Diesel Difference   21
  Getting Repairs Out of Town   22
  If You Have to Go Back   23

Communicating With Your Mechanic   25
  Speaking the Language   27
  Questions for Your Mechanic   29
  Getting a Second Opinion   31
  What Your Mechanic Would Like to Tell You   33
  Describe the Symptoms   34
  Don't Expect to Borrow Tools   36
  Be a Good "Comeback"   37
  Mechanics' Horror Stories   39
  Resolving Complaints the Easy Way   40
  Keep Good Warranty Records   42
  Waiting for Parts   43
  Your Day in Court   45
  Some Good News Stories   47

Understanding Your Car   49
  Thermostat: The Cooling System's Gatekeeper   51
  What Does Horsepower Really Mean?   52
  Identifying Your Engine   54
  Air: Filtering, Turbocharging, and Carbureting   56

Under the Hood: Wires and Belts   58
Some Disclosures About Distributors   60
Automatic Action: Transmissions and Chokes   62
Power: Steering and Brakes   64
Your Emission Control System   66
Your Fuel Filter Can Let You Down   69
Take Care of Your Tires   70

Keeping It Going   **73**

Oil: Your Car's Lifeblood   75
Transmissions: Preventing an Expensive Repair   77
Water: Keeping Your Engine Cool   78
Gas Up Right and Keep the Lead Out   80
Checking Your MPG   82
Octane Ratings: What Do They Mean?   83
Gasoline Alternatives   85
Brakes, Belts, Steering and Keeping Cool   86
Battery Basics: Keeping the Juice Flowing   88
Keep on Top of Your Tires   90
Extending the Life of Your Car   91
Special Care for the "Middle-Aged" Car   93
Your Tool Kit   95
The Undriven Vehicle   97
Wash and Wax   98

What's Wrong When...   **101**

Your Car Won't Start   103
Your Car Stalls or Backfires   106
S-T-O-P: A-OK!   107
You Have Carburetor Problems   109
The Steering Wheel Vibrates   110
Your Engine Overheats   112
Your Fan Stops—or Won't Stop   113
Your Brakes Are Making Noise   114
Gasoline Is Leaking   116
Engine Power Loss, Headlight Failure or Fire   117
Your Steering Wheel Pulls to One Side   119

Ripoff Tipoffs   **121**

Advertised Specials   123
"Can't Tell the Cost Until We Tear Into It"   124
Ask to See the Test   125
"Guaranteed to Improve Your Mileage"   126
Don't Let the Guarantee Rip You Off   127
Beware of Counterfeit Parts   128
A Shocking Discovery   129
Emergency Repairs: A Long Distance Ripoff Tipoff   130
"Don't Worry—They All Do That"   132
Repair Protection by Credit Card   133

4

Myths And Mysteries 135

Tuneup Tales and Legends 137
Carburetor Misconceptions 139
Carburetor Fables That Can Cost You 141
The Bad Load of Gas 143
Leaded Gasoline Is Better 145
The 85 MPG Car 147
The Catalytic Converter Test Pipe Scam 149
Tales of Transmission Fluid and Timing Belts 150
Slow Down: With Brakes or Engine? 151

You Can Do It Yourself! 153

Getting Help 156
Safety and Tool Tips 158
Buying Parts 160
Pre-Trip Inspection and Winterizing 162
Replacing Wiper Inserts and Checking Tire Pressure 164
Caring for Vinyl 166
Changing Light Bulbs 167
Opening a Frozen Lock 168
Changing a Tire 169
Changing Your Air Filter 170
Replacing Your Car's Battery 171
Changing the Engine Oil 173

Index 174

ACKNOWLEDGEMENTS

The Armchair Mechanic represents much more than two authors putting on paper their collective wisdom about auto repair. Many others contributed to the effort and each of us would like to acknowledge those folks who helped us individually and collectively

From Tom Kelly: Much of the information in *The Armchair Mechanic* was acquired as the result of "hands-on" experience. Some was passed onto me by colleagues or competitors, including Alan Coombs, the best mechanic I have ever known; George Ottoson, a former officer of the Washington State Automotive Service Councils; Bill Earp (A relative of the Marshall!) who knows more about transmissions than anyone. Gratitude goes to the radio stations, advertising agencies, and sponsors who supported "Tom Kelly, Your Master Mechanic," especially Spectrum Advertising, WHP, and Francis For Ford of Harrisburg, my longest-standing sponsor. Special appreciation is expressed to my wife, Lenore, who gave me the original idea for the radio series, and who corrected all 600 scripts.

Thanks are due to David Cokely who, as Operations Manager of KING Radio in Seattle, placed the series on that station, and to KING Radio producer Jessica Baldwin, who introduced me to Jack Gillis!

From Jack Gillis: The Armchair Mechanic would have been merely a great idea if it were not for the long hours and hard work put into preparing the manuscript by my research assistant Karen Fierst and researcher Cristina Mendoza. Special thanks go to graphic designer Susan Cole and ace typesetter Ray Weiss and the staff of Lithographics. The efforts of Teresa Wooten-Talley, Sherri Soderberg Pittman, Sherrie Good and David Smith were important ingredients in the success of this project. We are also indebted to John Michel of Harper & Row for his editorial vision and our agent Stuart Krichevsky. My personal appreciation goes to Tom Kelly, a patient, honest and bright man. Finally, but most importantly, special thanks to my wife Marilyn and little Brian Brennan Gillis who waited until the manuscript was delivered.

For Lenore and Marilyn

INTRODUCTION

This book is not designed for the car repair buff or the back yard mechanics, but for the average car owner who simply wants to save money on repairs, communicate with a mechanic and avoid being the needless victim of a repair rip-off. It's for people concerned about keeping their biggest purchase in top shape.

Whether you read this book front to rear, rear to front, or at random, you will soon notice that this is *not* a "how to" book. It's a "when to" and "whether to" book, intended for leisurely, clean-knuckled perusal while you're comfortable in your favorite reading chair. It's your guide to becoming an *Armchair Mechanic!*

If you're a do-it-yourselfer, *The Armchair Mechanic* will provide you an overview plus some information you may otherwise have had to learn the hard way. If you take all your work to a professional mechanic, this book will help you understand his language and give you a special perspective on his viewpoint. To get the best repairs you need a good mechanic, *The Armchair Mechanic* is a complete "tool box" of techniques, tips and tales on getting your car repaired. It will give you the information you need to:

- Understand what may be wrong with your car;
- Communicate with a mechanic;
- Insure that repairs were necessary and done correctly;
- Save money and aggravation by getting the right repair done for the right price.

When you have the worrisome suspicion that your car needs fixing, it is a safe bet that you will feel a gnaw of apprehension. *The*

Armchair Mechanic will help you get automobile repairs without being cheated, and without worrying about being cheated.

Even if you intend never to work on your car, you can profit from learning about it. Before you go on a trip, for example, asking your mechanic for a "tuneup" can easily cost you $100 more than a "checkup." Worse yet, while you may need the "checkup," it's likely you do not need the "tuneup." Just knowing the language will help you save on repairs.

There *are* steps you can take to protect yourself against dishonesty, incompetence, misunderstanding, and unrealistic expectations. And that's what *The Armchair Mechanic* is all about.

The first step in getting good repairs is *Finding a Good Mechanic* so that's the first section in the book. In spite of popular wisdom, there are thousands of good mechanics; the problem is in finding them. Here's everything you need to evaluate a mechanic and make a choice that will satisfy your car repair problems without depleting your wallet.

After you've found a mechanic you'll need to know how to speak the language. That's what *Communicating with a Mechanic* is all about—learning to talk about your car and its problems. We've also included some things your mechanic would like to tell you because, after all, communication is a two-way street. And finally, there are tips on how to solve problems when the communication breaks down.

The third chapter is on *Understanding Your Car.* With nearly 10,000 parts, it's no wonder most of us feel intimidated at the prospect of learning how a car works. Fear not, this section breaks the car down, system by system, so anyone can understand the basics. Understanding how your car works is essential to keeping it in good health and getting the best repairs for your dollar.

Keeping It Going will help you stay on the road and out of the repair shop. Spending as little as fifteen minutes a month on your car can make one of the most expensive products you own last longer. Here's everything you need to do to keep it going.

Rarely will an automobile have a catastrophic problem without giving us some warning. The problem is that we don't always recognize or sometimes ignore the warning signals. *What's Wrong When . . .* gives you the inside story on what your car may be trying to tell you. Paying attention to those signals will save you money.

Ripoff Tipoffs gives you the inside information on avoiding repair scams. Most mechanics are honest, but we've all had the experience of wondering if we really needed that repair. In the car repair world you don't have to be on guard all the time, especially if you know the *ripoff tipoffs*. A *ripoff tipoff* may help you find a reliable repair shop, or appreciate a good mechanic when you do find him.

America's love affair with the automobile has generated many *Myths and Mysteries*. When it comes to cars, all is not as it seems. These stories will help you avoid inadvertently damaging your car by adhering to a folk legend.

We've also included a section on doing your own repairs. Yes, *You Can Do It Yourself*. This chapter will get you started with the most basic of do-it-yourself tasks for the beginner. We don't expect you to change your transmission, but if you want, you can certainly change your oil.

Finally, if you find a word or phrase that you don't understand, check it out in the *Index*. We don't expect you to sit down and read the book from cover to cover, so use the *Index* to help you zero-in on car problems as they arise.

Each of the items in *The Armchair Mechanic* is designed to be read and understood in just a few minutes. To get the most out of the book, go through a few sections at a time and keep it around as a handy reference. Hopefully, it will be your best "tool" for keeping your car healthy and your pocketbook happy.

About the Book and the Authors

This book began as a series of 600 ninety second radio shows written by Tom Kelly for his syndicated program called *Tom Kelly, Your Master Mechanic*. Tom has had a combined broadcasting and auto repair career that spans over forty years. As a highly experienced mechanic, he has gained certification from the National Institute for Automotive Service Excellence in Engine Rebuilding, Engine Performance (Tuneup), Electrical Systems, and Heating and Air conditioning. Not only a hands on mechanic, Tom has owned and operated an auto repair business.

Tom met Jack Gillis, author of *The Car Book*, when he interviewed Jack for a radio program in Seattle, Washington. As a consumer advocate, Jack has written and edited a number of consumer guides including *The Used Car Book, How to Make Your Car Last Almost Forever, The Bank Book, The Childwise Catalog: A Consumer Guide to Buying the Best and Safest Products for Your Children, How to Fly: The Consumer Federation of America's Airline Survival Guide* and he is a columnist for *Good Housekeeping Magazine*.

After the radio interview in 1984, Tom and Jack met for a few hours over coffee and discussed the many problems consumers had getting car repairs. Thus, *The Armchair Mechanic* was born. A combination of a trained mechanic's years of experience with a consumer advocate's sensitivity to the problems consumers face in getting car repairs. Tom and Jack bring very different perspectives to this all consuming issue and you will note that throughout the book, each contributes his specific advice and experiences in the form of side comments.

Tom continues to live near Seattle in Mountlake Terrace, Washington with his wife Lenore. His syndicated radio program is still on the air and he is working on a new book called *How to Date Miss Universe*. Jack lives in Washington, DC with his wife Marilyn and three children. He is currently the Director of Public Affairs for the Consumer Federation of America.

Jack and Tom are also working on their next book, *The Armchair Mechanic Looks Under the Hood*.

FINDING A GOOD MECHANIC

Despite popular wisdom, today's cars are built better and are more reliable than ever before. Unitized bodies, MacPherson strut suspension, computerized ignition, fuel injection, and self-diagnostics all mean that today's cars require less maintenance. But when they do need service, they demand the attention of a highly skilled, extensively trained, and well-paid technician. So the first tool an armchair mechanic needs is a good mechanic—a "family practice" kind of technician who can take care of most of the automobile's ills, and who will send it to a specialist if needed.

Naturally, communication is vital. But it takes time to build rapport with your mechanic, and it requires a good, two-way relationship. So, when you're evaluating your mechanic's other qualifications, ask yourself if you like him. At the beginning, be cautious that you're not dealing with a charming scoundrel. But be aware that the mechanic is sizing you up as well. Any mechanic will assure you that there are also customers who are con artists.

The technology of the automobile just won't stand still. As soon as mechanics are familiar with distributors with no points or condensers, along come newer distributors controlled by onboard computers, followed by ignition systems with no distributors at all! A body shop buys state-of-the-art equipment for straightening frames, then cars are built that have no frames. Drive wheels move from rear to front, and all the old, familiar steering and suspension components are changed. All of these changes have a "ripple effect" on the other parts of the car. The result: every advance in technology is accompanied by new challenges in training mechanics—and new challenges in finding good mechanics.

Your regular mechanic should practice his specialties and should know where his expertise ends. Today, because automobiles have become so sophisticated, more and more mechanics specialize in just one system of a car, maybe the transmission, the brakes, the ignition, the engine, or the body.

One thing is for sure—shopping around can pay off. Don't necessarily go for the lowest price. A good rule of thumb is to eliminate the highest and lowest estimates. The mechanic with the highest is probably charging too much and the one with the lowest may be cutting too many corners.

If you can visit the shop, take a look around. A well-kept shop is a sign of pride in workmanship. This has nothing to do with whether the waiting room is carpeted or air-conditioned or serves fresh coffee, but whether the mechanic's work space is reasonably neat and organized. A skilled and efficient mechanic would probably not be working in a messy shop.

Chances are, the mechanic you are dealing with is a good one, but if you have any questions, or simply need to find a good auto technician, this section will help you find the best.

"Good mechanics and good customers tend to gravitate toward each other, so one way for you to find a good mechanic is to be a good customer.

A good customer makes appointments in advance, keeps them on time, discusses symptoms with the technician, makes an effort to understand what the mechanic proposes to do, and takes time to watch any testing attentively. A shop reserves a service bay and a technician's time for that appointment, and if the customer is a no-show, the shop is unlikely to reserve room for that customer in the future. A good mechanic routinely puts his diagnosis in writing and provides a firm estimate of repair costs in advance." T.K.

Choosing a Repair Shop

At first glance the choices for car care may seem bewildering. They include: neighborhood "garage" or service stations (general repairs); specialty shops (works only on specific items—brakes, radiators, transmissions, tuneups, etc.); new car dealers (complete service for a particular manufacturer's line); national chains (specialty or general repair); and regional franchises (nationally advertised, locally owned). Within each category there are all kinds of subdivisions, for example, the "leased service department," where you think you're dealing with a nationally known chain only to discover at crunch time that the service department is operated by a tenant!

There are excellent repair facilities to be found in each category. Try to find a shop close to where you live or work.

Here are two tricks you can use to bring out the best in any shop:

1. Let the shop owner or manager know that when you find a good basic mechanic you intend to be a regular, repeat customer. Tell the mechanic if someone else in your family owns a car and who referred you. Now, the shop owner will not only want to make a favorable impression on you, but also on that other customer who referred you.

2. When you're satisfied that the shop has treated you well, and that you can confidently recommend it to others, be sure to do so, and ask your friends to mention your name. You'll become a source of additional business, a VIP customer they won't want to lose. They'll knock themselves out to please you!

A specialty shop is a repair facility that services only one or two systems on a vehicle. Often brakes and front suspensions will be serviced at a single shop, which may frequently sell, install, and balance tires. Mufflers

"I never worked on automatic transmissions. But I know the honest, moderately priced transmission shops and the few ripoffs in my area. I'd never mention the bad guys by name, but I often referred customers to the good guys." T.K.

"That kind of advice from a regular mechanic who values your repeat business will save you money." J.G.

13

and radiators, or, more properly, exhaust systems and cooling systems, seem to be a popular, if illogical combination.

Like a regular repair shop, a specialty shop may be a one-location, locally owned and managed operation, part of a franchise organization, or a member of a regional or national chain. Many car owners patronize them, and these days even service departments of some new car dealerships farm out some of their work to specialty shops.

One advantage of specialty shops is that, because they only work on one or two systems of the car, they do it well and less expensively. However, before settling on a major repair such as a new transmission or complete brake overhaul, compare the price with your regular mechanic to be sure you're getting the best deal. Tip: Beware of special deals offered by national chain specialty shops. Often those "free" shock absorbers come with fifty to seventy-five dollars worth of additional parts and labor.

Certification: What Is It?

The really competent mechanic—the one you want to work on your car—is a technician in continuous training. (It's estimated that today's mechanics must spend ten hours a week training just to stay even.)

Check the credentials of any mechanic who works on your vehicle. Only a handful of states *require* a mechanic to prove proficiency before being allowed to work on your car. What you're looking for is recent recertification and fresh retraining diplomas. There are plenty of opportunities for technician retraining. Trade schools do a good job. Parts manufacturers, through their warehouses and representatives, are conducting more clinics, as are manufacturers of test equipment. Fortunately, there is an alternative to government licensing of automotive technicians. The National Institute for Automotive Service Excellence, founded in 1972, established a voluntary mechanic's certification program based on experience requirements plus the passing of written tests. Today, over 216,000 mechanics, including 516 women, have passed the written test in at least one category.

There are some limitations built into the Automotive Service Excellence (ASE) certification program. The *shop* is never certified, only individual mechanics. A technician experienced and qualified in only *one* specialty is entitled to wear the shoulder patch of an "ASE Certified Automobile Technician." A mechanic who qualified as an engine technician may not be a good choice to work on your brakes. There are also some mechanics who choose not to be tested. The result is that not all excellent mechanics are certified. Neither are all certified mechanics excellent; some are marginally qualified by experience and may have "squeaked by" one single written test.

"I remember an incident when a customer nudged me, winked knowingly, nodded toward a young mechanic and said, 'Don't let the kid work on my car, okay?' The "kid" in this case was a youthful looking 33-year-old with four years of vocational high school, countless postsecondary classes and clinics, fifteen years of good experience, and every automotive certification that exists!" T.K.

15

There are eight automobile specialties. They are Engine Repair, Engine Performance, Automatic Transmission/Transaxle, Manual Drive Train and Axle, Suspension and Steering, Brakes, Electrical Systems, and Heating and Air Conditioning. The gold-lettered patch that reads "ASE Certified Master Auto Technician" is worn by a technician certified in all eight categories.

Automobiles change mighty fast. The mechanic who learned his trade twenty years ago, but then stood still, may be perfectly competent to work on cars of the Sixties, but he'd be lost on computerized ignition, anti-lock brakes, fuel injection, or any of the dramatic breakthroughs of the past twenty years. ASE certification is good for five years. The mechanic you want, will be certified.

Remember: A repair shop may display a sign indicating that they have ASE certified mechanics, but will have only one mechanic certified in one area. Make sure that the person working on your car is certified *and* certified in the repair you need.

Certification Sign

For Good Repairs, Find a Good Diagnostician

With today's marvelous new test equipment, one might suspect that the diagnostic technician is no longer needed. Not true! As cars have become more complicated and sophisticated, so has test equipment. It requires an expert technician to hook it up, make the right test, and interpret the results. If a knocking noise in an engine is coming from a worn fuel pump, all the engine tests in the world will never find it until the diagnostician decides to test the fuel pump.

In a large shop, the diagnostician supervises the testing and assigns the repair work to the right mechanic. So don't worry if one technician performs your testing and shuffles your car to another service bay where a different mechanic does the work. The separation of the two jobs minimizes the shop's operating costs and contributes to keeping your bill as low as possible.

Test, Don't Guess

The phrase that *experienced* mechanics repeat over and over to themselves and drum into the brains of apprentices is one that every automobile owner should commit to memory: *Test, don't guess.*

The competent and honest shop will almost always test before the mechanic starts to work. Be prepared to pay a reasonable fee for testing, but agree in advance what the fee will be. Ask that the tests be explained to your satisfaction in nontechnical language. Understanding the test results is important. Often, you must make repair decisions based on those results. The good shop will give you a definite diagnosis in writing.

In the past, when the cost of testing was much lower, the shop absorbed the expense as part of its overhead, rather than itemizing it for the customer. Today, shops charge their

"There are a number of comparisons between medicine and mechanics. An emergency room performs the same kind of screening on humans as a diagnostic bay in a large repair shop does on cars. A heart monitor actually resembles an automotive scope. On the other hand, the old-time mechanic at the corner station and the general practitioner of medicine, both of whom worked wonders with a minimum of equipment and a maximum of experience, are now vanishing breeds."
T.K.

customers separately for testing, and this works to the customer's advantage. Let's say you have an engine problem that may be caused by bad or poorly adjusted valves. Replacing the valves can cost you $300; the adjustment may cost thirty dollars. The precise testing to tell the difference may cost you twenty dollars or so—a good investment. The shop earns a proper return from its investment in test equipment and the customer gets the right job the first time.

In addition to pinpointing the exact repair the vehicle requires, the test equipment also allows your mechanic to test again to be sure the work was done fully and correctly. That's the important two-step process—doing the right job and doing the job right. Find a shop that subscribes to this process, and you'll be a contented customer.

There's a distinction between testing, for which you'll be expected to pay, and the preservice interview. That's the question-and-answer session when you first arrive at the shop, for which there should be no charge. The distinction can become fuzzy when you consider that at many shops the interview and testing are done by the same person, and many shops don't charge for simple tests.

The rule of thumb is that you should not expect to pay a fee until test equipment is actually applied to your vehicle, and then the fee should be based on the amount of time the testing takes and the complexity of the equipment required. It will cost you more to have your wheel alignment tested than to have your voltage regulator checked out. A complete scope diagnosis and exhaust analysis may take up to forty-five minutes and will cost up to 75 percent of the shop's hourly rate.

Watch for advertised specials. Shops frequently offer testing for free or at greatly reduced prices. They hope that if they find a problem you'll have them do the repair work. Be sure you ask how much each test will cost *before* testing begins.

The bedrock basic is this: For every problem an automobile can have, there is a test procedure to prove it and a piece of test equipment to perform it.

How Much Should It Cost?

Car repairs are expensive. Automotive parts cost more than they did even a few years ago. Service procedures are more tedious, more complex, and more time-consuming. Some of today's complex cars require more sophisticated tools and test equipment. Hourly shop rates have escalated to reflect inflationary pressures, including insurance, rent, utilities, taxes, and mechanics' wages. So, how do you know what the correct charges should be? Communicating with your technician and understanding your bill are two important components in avoiding a ripoff.

Your repair bill has two sections: parts and labor. The shop will charge you the list price for parts, which is higher than the dealer price. You could buy similar parts for less at a discount parts store. The repair shop carries a comparatively small inventory, and has to account for the cost of going to the parts store to pick up parts. Rather than itemize for this service, most shops simply charge list price. It's still a good buy, because it includes a warranty. Should any of them fail, the parts and labor to reinstall them are usually guaranteed by the shop.

The labor charge on the bill includes the shop's hourly rate times the length of time required for your job. This is usually determined by a reference book called a flat-rate manual. These manuals list hundreds of repairs for hundreds of cars and the approximate time each should take. The hourly labor rate should be posted. If it's not, ask. Don't hesitate to question a labor charge. An identical procedure may take three or four times as long in one car as in a different model of the same make. Because the listings may be only a single line apart, in a book three inches thick, mechanics occasionally read the wrong line.

"A verbal estimate is not worth the paper it's written on." T.K.

19

Even the most honest technician can make this kind of error, but will correct it. The good shops won't mind your asking, and most will pleasantly show you the item in the flat-rate book. They understand that most car owners don't mind paying a fair price for quality workmanship.

The Written Estimate

Most consumers underestimate, by a large factor, the cost of automotive service. The good shop, like any enterprise, is after repeat business and knows that one way to lose a customer's future business is to confront the customer after the fact with a bill larger than expected.

That's why the well-run shop automatically reaches for a repair order while the customer is still present. The mechanic looks up the prices of parts that will be needed and writes them on the repair order for the customer to see. Labor time is added, a total is taken, and a copy of the estimate is given to the customer. A good shop routinely furnishes a written estimate in advance and usually asks the customer to sign it. A wise customer demands one before authorizing work. This prevents the "five o'clock surprise."

The Diesel Difference

Finding a good repair shop that works on diesel-powered cars can be a problem. Performing a tuneup on a diesel, checking injectors and spray patterns, even checking the timing, requires different equipment and training than for gasoline engines. However, there are plenty of shops that are well-equipped, thoroughly trained, and fully experienced on automotive diesels.

Dealers who sell diesels are one option. Finding a qualified *independent* is a bit tougher. There is something in the personality makeup of many good mechanics that tends to make them poor promoters. Also, the shop that's really good has a clientele that grows by word of mouth, until the mechanics are doing all the work they think they can handle.

If you are looking for a diesel-engine shop, ask your regular mechanic first. He may surprise you and indicate that he has trained his mechanics and bought the test equipment for diesel work—more and more mechanics are doing so. Otherwise, he may recommend a nearby shop. Also, ask your friends who own diesels and watch the small ads in neighborhood or want-ad newspapers.

When you find a diesel shop, apply the usual standards. Observe and understand the tests, get a firm written estimate before authorizing work, look for certified technicians, and understand your guarantee. In these matters, your diesel is *exactly* like a gasoline car!

"Really good mechanics are often poor promoters—so finding a good specialist takes some looking." J.G.

Getting Repairs Out of Town

There are horrendous tales of motorists stranded in strange cities who've been badly cheated by unscrupulous mechanics out to fleece the tourists. While many of these stories are exaggerated, the auto repair industry has its share of bad apples. Here are some ways to prevent being taken for a ride.

If there's a regional or national chain back home that has always treated you well, look for a branch in this city. Call a friend, acquaintance, or business customer for a local recommendation. Often tourist information bureaus will have a list of reputable repair shops. Ask around at noncompeting businesses—restaurants, barber shops, clothing stores—for the name of a reputable shop. Whatever your source, mention it when you first meet your strange mechanic, to let him know why you chose his shop.

When judging an unfamiliar shop, first impressions do count, so you'll probably want to select a shop that's businesslike in appearance, neat, and clean. Be wary of quick decisions, snap judgments, and anything that hints at pressure to perform costly repairs—at your expense. During the preservice interview, be alert to the desirable suggestion that testing may be required to identify your exact problem. Mechanics are not miracle workers; no one can repair a car until its problems are identified. As always, be sure you understand the results of any testing that's needed.

Get a written diagnosis of your trouble, a firm written estimate before you authorize *any* repairs, and a guarantee. These procedures won't assure that you'll find a great shop. But if all the indicators are right, you've shifted the odds in your favor.

If You Have to Go Back

One way to identify how good a repair shop really is by observing the way it handles a "comeback." A comeback is the mechanic's jargon for a car that has come back to the shop with the same complaint as on a previous visit.

A good repair shop is one that acts just as glad to see you as a comeback as it was when you were a new customer. Good shops will have someone who will listen attentively to your question or problem. They will *not* try to brush you off. Often a test drive will help pinpoint the problem, so if the shop's representative doesn't suggest it, you should. Another alternative is to put the car back on the test equipment. A good shop will offer to do this at its expense.

The ideal shop is going to look upon the comeback as a sales opportunity. They may easily, and at no charge, answer your question or resolve your complaint and thereby sell you solidly on the quality of their service.

As a customer, you can earn a positive response by coming back as soon as you have a question or notice a problem. In fact, if possible budget time for this contingency. The shop will be *much* more understanding and cooperative after thirty minutes than after thirty days. If you take the attitude that "we have a problem to solve together," you'll get the best results. Don't be accusatory the first time back.

"Let me give you an insider's tip on a ploy you can use to guarantee a speedy response to repair problems. Once in a while, when you're especially pleased with a shop's work, you might drive back and tell them what a good job they did. They get so few customers who take the time to do that, I promise they'll remember you favorably next time. And that's like money in the bank!" T.K.

COMMUNICATING WITH YOUR MECHANIC

One of the main reasons there are so many complaints about auto repairs is because of simple failures of communication between the customer and the mechanic. Communicating with a mechanic is not necessarily hard to do. In fact, most mechanics are more than willing to explain a needed repair or necessary procedure. One important rule of thumb: If the mechanic cannot explain problems to your satisfaction or understanding, then you should probably take your business elsewhere.

This chapter contains some tips on talking with your mechanic. We have presented it in three sections. The first three items offer some basic tips on communicating with your mechanic. The second five items look at car repair from your mechanic's perspective—*what your mechanic would like to tell you.* Finally, despite all of our efforts and good intentions, there will be those situations when seemingly insurmountable problems arise, so the final three items offer some tips on resolving those problems and tips on complaining.

As a customer, you're entitled to competence, honesty, and a professional attitude that includes courtesy and a concern for your problems. Remember to offer these same traits to your mechanic. Be as detailed as possible in describing your car's problems. Explain *all* the symptoms until you're sure you are understood. Invest your time to go on a test drive if one is recommended. Authorize reasonable testing. Be totally honest about how long the difficulty has existed and how severe it has been. Don't just settle for a written estimate; be sure you understand it and know what to expect from the repairs. Ask if you need more work than discussed, or if less will do. Realistic expectations and good communication will help insure that you are an informed and contented customer.

Remember, your mechanic is not a mind-reader and doesn't know what kind of service you want until you tell him. Telling the mechanic that you intend to sell or trade your car in six months may suggest a different repair procedure than if you plan to keep the car for years.

There are more consumer complaints about automobile repairs than any other category. That means that the auto service industry has a tendency to produce unhappy customers at a rate faster than any other business. Whatever the reasons for these regrettable problems, the information in this chapter will help you avoid being the victim.

"Don't be afraid to use your own instincts when sizing up a mechanic. One of the best ways a mechanic can inspire confidence is by being a good listener. If you sense a good rapport with the mechanic, chances are that you will have fewer problems down the road. If you find yourself dealing with a mechanic with whom you have difficulty establishing communication, or who you simply don't like—take your car to a different shop!" J.G.

Speaking the Language

Part of working with your mechanic is learning to speak some of the language and being able to describe the *symptoms* of your car's problems.

The shop you choose to patronize regularly should be one that has a manager with whom you can communicate easily and comfortably. Different people use different styles of communicating and you want a shop where you feel comfortable. When you don't understand something, ask again. Posted prices, written guarantees, prior estimates, and patient preservice interviews are all signs that the mechanic is willing to communicate.

Your biggest responsibility is to *describe* symptoms accurately. It's important to focus on the symptoms because you don't want to send the mechanic off on the wrong, and possibly more expensive, track. For example, don't say, "The car 'shimmies' at high speeds. Please give me a front end alignment." Just tell about the "shimmy": All you may need is an inexpensive tire balancing.

Try to learn what an engine sounds like when it's cranking but not starting, and how that differs from the clicking sound that happens when you turn the key and the battery is low. Ask your mechanic what it sounds like when a drive unit fails to engage and runs free. That knowledge may save you hard cash. Learn the difference between a brake pad wear sensor and the harsh metal-to-metal sound of a worn-out brake shoe. In the one case you can drive safely to a brake shop, in the other, you should have the car towed because you may cause serious damage or have a bad accident. Knowing the difference can save you money—and maybe your life.

When it comes to testing, you may be asked to stay out of the testing area. However, insist

"The right mechanic will help you learn to speak his language, maybe not like a native, but at least like a well-prepared tourist." T.K.

on observing the testing for your financial protection. After all, it's your money that's going to pay for the repairs. A distinction is usually made between test area and work area, though in very small shops they're the same space. Those smaller shops should allow you to watch the tests and should explain them until you understand. But when the testing is over and the work begins, expect to be asked to leave. For the mechanic's physical protection, as well as your own, be understanding and cooperative when you're asked to wait in the waiting room. Some waiting rooms provide windows to the work area so you can observe safely from a distance.

Here are some tips on communicating with your mechanic:

• Be as specific as possible about the work you want done. Statements such as "Fix whatever is wrong," or "Repair as required" invite misunderstanding. There is a big price difference between a tuneup and replacing the spark plugs.

• Be totally candid in discussing finances. Insist on knowing, in writing, how much a job will cost for parts, labor, and taxes. This is particularly important when you will be having three or four repairs done at the same time. Often, this is not an all-or-nothing decision. Ask the mechanic to list priorities; those repairs needed at once, those that can safely wait a short while, and those that may be put off for an even longer time. With this information, you can budget your repairs over a period of months. A good shop will be happy to do this in order to get a steady, repeat customer.

Questions for Your Mechanic

As a customer, you have the right to ask for an explanation of every statement your mechanic makes. Asking is most important after you've been given a diagnosis. Automotive technicians sometimes use jargon that they understand, but which you may not. Unless you are absolutely certain about what they are talking about, it is vital that you ask for more information.

For example, after completing tests on your vehicle, a mechanic may report, "I'm afraid we found a bad PCV," or "Your EGR needs to be replaced," or "You have a defective CCU." They're all three initials, so they must all cost about the same, right? Wrong! Replacing the PCV will cost around ten dollars; the EGR could run $100; and the CCU may produce a bill for over $1000. If you sign a blank repair order or say "Go ahead and fix it," you have authorized the repair! Asking the right questions will help you be certain the repair is necessary and avoid an unpleasant surprise with the final bill.

The Preservice Interview

The *preservice interview* is often the first contact between car owner and repair shop. During the preservice interview, tell the mechanic everything you can about your car's problem. If you have written notes, that's great. Don't try to diagnose the causes; simply report the symptoms.

First impressions do count, and a good shop is likely to be orderly and inviting. It will have someone who listens to you attentively, asks questions, and answers yours before starting work. If you don't like what happens during that introductory interview, take your car elsewhere.

Many people avoid preservice interviews or

"Before taking my car in for service I jot down all the items I want checked on a piece of paper. This reminds me to tell the service manager everything I want done. Before I leave, I tape the list to the steering wheel. The mechanic who works on my car may notice something on the list that the service manager forgot to tell him." J.G.

endure them as a kind of unhappy penance. Your responsibility in the preservice interview is to *ask questions and plenty of them.* For example, if you take your car in for a tuneup and you're asked, "Major or minor?" be certain to find out the difference. Those words are defined differently by different shops, and at some places the difference is well over a hundred dollars!

What you don't want to do is misdirect the mechanic, to send him looking, for example, for a complex suspension problem, when all you may have is an underinflated tire. As a given symptom can be produced by a dozen different causes, the good technician will start by considering the easiest and fastest repair items, which also means the least expensive. It is worth re-emphasizing that to help him do this, simply describe the symptoms and only the symptoms. Explain how the car is misbehaving and let the mechanic determine the causes!

Here are the four questions you should ask any mechanic who ever works on your car:
- What does that mean?
- How much will that cost?
- Is this repair certain to solve the problem?
- Is there a less expensive satisfactory solution?

Copy these questions onto a little card and keep it in your glove box.

When you find a mechanic who listens attentively to your questions and answers them in language you can understand, be glad you found his shop. If your regular mechanic treats you well, reward him with your future patronage.

Getting a Second Opinion

Before you spend several hundred dollars on a major repair, it may pay to get a second opinion.

There are two specific reasons why getting a second opinion is a good idea. First, you may be dealing with a dishonest mechanic and second, an honest mechanic can make a mistake. If a shop won't allow you to watch their testing, or explain the testing in non-technical language until you understand it, get a second opinion. If they won't put their diagnosis in writing, *always* get a second opinion.

Be prepared to pay for a second opinion. Of course, it would be foolish to spend thirty dollars trying to avoid a twenty dollar job, but there are errors made by careless or hurried technicians. Let's assume that a gasket between your carburetor and intake manifold has eroded. You observe and understand the tests that prove a leak. You're told that a new carburetor, for $250 installed, will eliminate the symptom, and so it will, because the new carburetor comes with a new gasket. That's when a second opinion can save you plenty: Replacing just the gasket will cost you about twenty-five dollars.

Here's how you protect yourself. *Consider* getting a second opinion if the cost of the repair is substantial or more than ten times the cost of the tests. *Always* get a second opinion if you don't understand the tests or can't get a diagnosis in writing. *Always* get a second opinion if you don't get an unequivocal answer to this question: "Is this the only kind of repair that can solve my problem?" Once in awhile, just being asked this question can motivate a conscientious technician to investigate more deeply, and to find that twenty-five dollar base gasket!

Before you get a second opinion for an *intermittent* problem consider this: Every mechanic has a favorite anecdote, usually from dearly acquired personal experience, about a car that would run just fine once it warmed up, but malfunctioned spectacularly when it was cold on first start-up in the morning.

There are at least two dozen factors that can cause or contribute to poor cold operation. The problem in troubleshooting is not so much that the mechanic does not know where to look; it's that there are so many places to look and sometimes only a few seconds to identify the cause before the engine starts to warm up and the problem disappears.

Still, some customers are understandably less than understanding when a mechanic says, "I'll have to keep your car overnight. If I don't find the problem first thing in the morning, I may have to keep the car for several days." As the unfortunate customer, if you ever have an intermittent problem, especially one related to cold operation, be prepared to be patient.

What Your Mechanic Would Like to Tell You

Five different managers of five different kinds of auto repair shops were once asked about their toughest customer problems. They all agreed that the worst problem was the "no show"—the customer who makes an appointment and then doesn't show up or phone to cancel. The reason the answers were so consistent is because this is a cost item over which the shop has no control.

In order to budget their time, most shops take reservations. Because of "no shows," they have to schedule more than they can handle to keep the mechanics busy. If you're told to bring your car in Tuesday and then told that it won't be ready until Thursday you're probably experiencing one result of the "no show" problem. If you're ever tempted to skip an appointment, at least call your mechanic and cancel. That way, you won't be part of the problem. Furthermore, some shops will be unlikely to reserve room for you in the future.

Here is a list of attributes good mechanics look for in their customers:

- A good customer makes appointments in advance and is on time.

- The good customer takes time to watch any testing attentively, discusses symptoms with the technician and makes an effort to understand what the mechanic proposes to do.

- The good customer has realistic expectations and realizes that the mechanic is a technician, not a miracle worker. A ten-year old car may never look or run like a current model.

- The good customer picks up the car and pays for the work as soon as it's finished.

- The good customer maintains a sense of perspective and, above all, maintains communication with the mechanic.

"If a new customer speaks ill of a previous shop, I assume that the customer had an unfortunate experience. If two previous shops were slandered, I assumed a borderline between bad luck and bad customer. If a customer condemns a third previous shop, I will assure him I couldn't possibly solve his problem and that it would take at least six months before I could work the car into my busy schedule." T.K.

Describe the Symptoms

Telling the mechanic too little can cost you. If all you say is, "My car is acting up," a busy or unwary mechanic may put the car on his exhaust analyzer, and charge you the cost for the test, only to learn the fuel system is working perfectly. If, on the other hand, you had said, "My car hesitates when I pull away from a stop," the mechanic would immediately have tested the timing advance unit. Complete cost of that simple test and repair would probably have been less than the unnecessary exhaust analysis.

Most mechanics agree that car owners can be victimized by unscrupulous repair shops. Most, however, also agree that the problem may be the fault of the owner. It is worth re-emphasizing that to avoid sending the mechanic off in the wrong direction and then having to pay for an unnecessary repair, describe all the symptoms.

Take, for example, the case of a customer who replaced his battery three times in less than two months. He went to three different shops where he simply directed each mechanic to install a new battery and never had the electrical system tested. The true problem could have been any number of items which could affect the battery and not the battery itself. If he had a regular mechanic and went back, he would not have had to buy the second battery. Furthermore, the chances are pretty good that if he had stated his original *problem*, rather than asking for a new battery, he probably wouldn't have had to buy a battery at all!

Another attitude mechanics hold is that most consumers underestimate, by a large factor, the predicted costs of automotive service. Automotive parts cost more than they did even a few years ago. Service procedures are more tedious, more complex, and more time

"The faster the mechanic solves your problem the less you pay and the sooner he goes on to his next customer. He makes more money by serving more customers and you pay less—you're both happy." T.K.

consuming. Hourly shop rates have escalated to reflect inflation, increases in rent, insurance, utilities, taxes, and mechanics' wages. However, the good shop is looking for repeat business and knows that one way to lose a customer's future business is to confront that customer, after the fact, with a bill larger than expected. That's why the well run shop automatically reaches for a repair order while the customer is still present.

They look up the prices of parts that will be needed and write them on the repair order for the customer to see. They will also include the cost of labor. A good shop routinely furnishes a written estimate in advance, and usually asks the customer to sign it.

Don't Expect to Borrow Tools

Another source of misunderstanding between the customer and mechanic is when an automobile owner asks a mechanic to borrow a tool and the mechanic refuses.

Mechanics have a number of good reasons for refusing to loan tools. Experience has taught them that loaned tools often disappear. The professional mechanic's version of a fairly common long-reach, half-inch combination wrench can cost about sixteen dollars. A ten-inch straight-blade screwdriver with a hardened tip can cost about the same. Most beginning mechanics suffer the loss of a dozen such items that "walk away," before they adopt a firm, lifelong policy of refusing to lend hand tools to anyone, including co-workers.

Another reason for mechanics' reluctance to loan tools is the risk of liability if a customer injures himself. For example, take the case of a mechanic who had lent a screwdriver to an old customer: The customer attempted a repair for which the screwdriver was the wrong tool, slipped, and gave himself a nasty gash in the wrist. After going to a hospital emergency room for treatment, the customer billed the charges to the mechanic. He then brought a lawsuit against the mechanic saying, in effect, "If he hadn't loaned me the screwdriver, I wouldn't have been injured." The customer didn't even return the screwdriver to the mechanic. He gave it to the attorney as evidence!

The happy solution is to carry a few of your own basic, familiar tools in your car. You can wrap them in an old towel, and tuck them in a corner of your trunk. If you must make a minor road repair, you'll have what you need. You won't have to ask to borrow a mechanic's tools and he won't have to turn you down.

"In most repair shops, the mechanics' tools are their own personal property. Their livelihood depends on this expensive investment. Missing tools often mean loss of income." J.G.

Be a Good "Comeback"

A "comeback" is the mechanic's word for a customer who comes back to the shop when he judges a repair was not done properly. Most good shops consider the comeback as an opportunity to cement relations with a customer, to resolve problems if they exist and sometimes to "sell" additional work, if that's what's required.

As the comeback customer you can do your part to be sure the shop stays on your side. Restrict the discussion to the mechanical facts and avoid personalities. "The wheel still seems to vibrate," will get you a cooperative response. "That stupid jerk messed up my car," invites a defensive rejection.

Recognize joint responsibility by using such diplomatic phrases as "We still have a problem," rather than the argumentative and threatening, "You have big trouble." Tact and good manners will always work wonders, but especially if you're the comeback customer.

The reams of publicity about dishonest mechanics are frustrating to those honest mechanics who have their own stories about dishonest customers. Every mechanic can tell you a story similar to this experience of Tom's: *A customer blustered into my shop an hour or so before closing time on a busy afternoon. He was the kind of comeback who could give comebacks a bad name. Positioning himself to be heard by customers in the crowded waiting room, he began to berate my lead mechanic, who had performed a tuneup on his car earlier in the day. "Come out and look at the old spark plugs you left in my car," he demanded. "I paid you for a tuneup, you charged me for eight brand new spark plugs, and the ones in my engine are old, used junk!"*

I checked with the lead mechanic who showed me the customer's old plugs in our trash bin. We both realized what happened. Our customer had swapped

"It's general industry practice to assume that all "comebacks" are honest unless proven otherwise, but believe me, there are dishonest customers!" T.K.

his new plugs with a friend, or removed them to store for future use, and was "working" us for a free set. I directed the customer to drive his car into a service bay, then closed and locked the bay door behind it. We installed the eight new plugs. I prepared a "no charge" service order, written in the form of a receipt for the plugs, and presented it to the customer for his signature. Abrasively, he refused. "In that case," I told him, "we won't be able to open the bay doors and release your car to you. And we leave for the night in fifteen minutes." He signed and left.

"Pretty clever," my lead mechanic said. He conned us out of eight free spark plugs." "True," I admitted, "but he can never be a comeback of ours again. He's conned himself out of a darned good shop—forever."

Mechanics' Horror Stories

Once in awhile, a car that won't run will be a tough challenge to any mechanic. Far more often, it is out of gas. That's the kind of owner's mistake that helps mechanics make a good living. Owners of automobiles make other mistakes around their cars, errors with terrifying danger potential.

Most mechanics are astounded at the condition of some cars driven by unwary owners who consider themselves safe drivers. Here are some experiences Tom actually encountered:

One time a small car came roaring into my shop. It had an automatic transmission and the idle had been set at 3000 RPM, so fast that the driver had to put the transmission in neutral in order to slow or stop. A shop had charged the customer to correct a condition in which the engine died in traffic. They "corrected" it all right, not by diagnosing and eliminating the problem, but by advancing the idle to a dangerously high speed that masked the problem. The mystery: Why did the owner pay his bill?

Another owner brought his car in because the brakes were grabbing a little. A little probing revealed that they grabbed so hard the car had done a compete 180-degree spinout in traffic, twice! And he drove it in! I've also heard drivers complain of "a little shimmy," when in fact they had a steel ball joint that was reduced to powder, or drive in with raw gasoline spraying onto a hot exhaust manifold, inviting a fire and explosion.

Don't become a mechanic's horror story. If your car is acting out of the ordinary, and you're not absolutely sure of yourself, telephone your regular mechanic and describe the symptoms. You may be reassured it's safe to drive or cautioned not to. In that case, a towing bill is cheaper than a breakdown, and far preferable to an accident or serious injury.

Resolving Complaints the Easy Way

The key to getting repair complaints resolved is to report any problems promptly. If you return to the shop in fifteen minutes, they'll attach far more importance to your complaint than if you wait fifteen days. If the trouble doesn't show up for fifteen days, it may be unrelated to the original work.

State your displeasure objectively and without flourishes. Invite cooperation, not debate. Invite the manager to take a test drive with you to observe the malfunction, enlist his professional troubleshooting ability. Be understanding if he declines, he may prefer to use test equipment. If he does test, it should be at the shop's expense. If all else fails, write a concise note outlining the facts and give it to the shop owner.

This is a time for good manners and a sense of proportion. If you say something like, "I wish you'd check my car. I'm not sure we solved the problem," you invite a cooperative response. If you shout, "This car ran better before you touched it and I'm going to sue," you're likely to incite resistance.

There have been entire books written on the subject of making effective complaints, and here are but a few tips. Organize in your mind exactly what your complaint is. A condemning "My car runs worse than when I brought it in," will predictably make the shop defensive. If you say, "I still feel a vibration in the front end," they're more likely to look for it with you.

Take your conflict to the person who can resolve it. At Joe's Garage, ask for Joe; at Smith Motors, you want Mr. Smith. The person whose name is on the business has the greatest interest in keeping the goodwill of all customers. Don't get in a tiff with the mechanic or foreman who worked on your car. He may have a mental block, or a vested interest in

"No one wants to be the type of person who goes through life asking for the manager. However, when it comes to disputes over auto repairs I can assure you that I would rather hear your complaint and be given an opportunity to resolve it, than lose your future business." T.K.

trying to prove he's right. Joe or Mr. Smith will act as referee and try to settle the differences.

Finally, decide what you want done, and state it clearly. The shop may suspect you're after an unjustified total refund when all you really want is to have the balance rechecked on your front wheels.

A reasonable, organized appeal to the owner, applied with courtesy, good manners, and a measure of good humor will often work wonders.

Keep Good Warranty Records

It's reasonable to expect a guarantee on car repairs. To make sure it sticks, get it in writing and save it!

Even though today's warranties have improved, they are still no better than your own record-keeping. When you buy a part for your car, your mechanic or parts store may add their own limited warranty, but essentially what you are getting is the warranty from the manufacturer of the part. The key to being able to benefit from these warranties is to keep good records and know, in advance, what's required to use the warranty.

For example, when your mechanic installs a set of new tires, he will usually give you your service order and a separate warranty certificate too. Before you leave the shop, make sure you understand the warranty. It may require that your mechanic note and sign the date and mileage of your car. If you buy an item from a parts store, the warranty may require that you mail in a registration or that you save the warranty certificate and a dated, itemized sales slip.

It's your responsibility to read, understand, and question warranties. The time to question the meaning of a guarantee is when you make the purchase. If a guaranteed tire fails, who pays for installation and balancing of the replacement? If a repair is guaranteed for the "life of the car," will there be parts, labor or service fees? Most guarantees of work done at a repair shop are valid only at the shop that did the work. If you have follow-up work done at a second shop, the first shop will usually *not* reimburse you. By complying with the terms of your warranty, you will have better protection. Remember: Save your documentation—if you lose your receipt, you lose your warranty!

"Whether in your glove box, a shoe box or elaborate filing system, saving your receipts is the only way to benefit from warranties" J.G.

42

Waiting for Parts

When your mechanic tells you he needs parts that are not available, this can result in irritating delays. First of all, it's in his shop's self-interest to have the part you need at the time you need it. To help with this goal, manufacturers and distributors have devised systems to determine how many and what kinds of parts are economical to carry in inventory. These are called "popularity codes." These codes range from *AAA* for the fastest moving items, through *AA, A, B, C,* and *D* for slow movers. *W* is for parts stocked only at the warehouse, *S* is a part available only on special order, and *O* is obsolete.

If your mechanic stocks one of a *D* item, and his warehouse stocks it ten deep, you're in for a delay if twelve people need that item on the same day, which does happen. That's what your mechanic means when he tells you, "The part you need is a *D* item, and the warehouse is out of stock."

You can beat the system by making appointments for service as far in advance as you can. Offer to leave a deposit for special order or low popularity parts. That way, your mechanic can start on your car as soon as it comes in. Unless, of course, your appointment is three weeks in advance, and there's a four-week delay for the parts.

If your car has been in the repair shop for what you believe is an inordinately long time and you've been told they are still waiting for parts, follow these steps to try to resolve the problem.

First, be reasonable when you contact the shop, and try to do so in person. Second, explain the problem to the person who has the authority to solve it—either the owner or the general manager. Then, describe exactly what you want. Suggest that you must have the car within a specified time, let's say, four hours, whether or not the repairs are completed. Pay for any work that's already done, and if parts really are back-ordered, offer to leave a deposit and agree to return to have them installed whenever they arrive. This way the ball will be in the manager's court.

If the problem is safety-related or such that you simply can't drive the car, then be understanding if the shop will not release it to you. No matter what the circumstances, try to be as pleasant and reasonable as possible. Take your complaint to someone who can act on it and tell the decision-maker what you want.

Your Day in Court

You feel your mechanic has ripped you off. You've tried all the alternatives, none of them have worked, and you're ready to sue. Here are some things to consider before you take this drastic action.

Consider offering a settlement. For example, ask for a refund on all or part of the labor portion of your bill. It may be unreasonable to expect a refund on new parts, since you're keeping the parts. However, many shops will offer a partial refund to settle a dispute they perceive as genuine.

Consider using an arbitration program. Arbitration is a relatively new method of resolving automobile repair problems. In most cases, both parties present their cases to a mediator or arbitration panel that decides on the merits of the complaint.

The benefit of arbitration is that it is somewhat informal, relatively speedy, and you do not need a lawyer to present your case. You may seek repairs, reimbursement for expenses, or a refund or replacement through these programs. Resolving a problem through arbitration is usually faster and less expensive than going to court.

The Better Business Bureau and the National Automobile Dealers Association run two of the most popular arbitration programs. You can call either the BBB or look up AUTOCAP in the telephone book. You can also contact your state attorney general's office for the names of other programs in your state.

The arbitration program will first attempt to mediate a resolution between you and the shop. If that doesn't work, your case will then be heard at an arbitration hearing.

Here are some tips to remember if you decide to use an arbitration program:

• Get a written description of how the

program works and make sure you understand the details before deciding to go to arbitration. Remember, the repair shop most likely has more experience with this than you do.

• Make sure the final decision is non-binding on you. If the decision is binding on you, you give up your right to appeal.

• Submit only *copies* of the material associated with your problem and make sure your documents are in *chronological order.*

No matter what course of action you take, you'll need facts: receipts, bills, cancelled checks, witnesses, exact dates, times, and amounts—anything that says the *facts* are on your side. Organize your facts and papers, which will be known as "exhibits," and present them. Don't write a speech to read, but do bring notes and refer to them often to be sure you don't leave out vital points. Be as brief as possible, but tell your whole story.

Presuming you have discussed the problem with the owner of the shop and were unable to reach a compromise, you might consider suing in a small claims court. Rules vary from one state to another, but you generally cannot have an attorney represent you. You *can* consult an attorney in advance, which is a good idea. However, if you and the mechanic are unable to resolve the problem it may mean the other side feels it has a strong case. You may be facing a tough battle in court or even a countersuit. In a countersuit the shop turns around and sues you for any money you may owe them.

Win, lose, or draw, after your day in court you'll know that your complaint has been judged by an impartial professional. If you win, you'll feel great. Even if you lose, it's a comfort to know you've given it your best shot.

Some Good News Stories

Not all difficulties between customer and mechanic have unhappy endings. Here is an offbeat example from Tom's personal experience.

I once had a customer whose poor, neglected car was in terrible shape. We rebuilt his carburetor, did a complete major tuneup, replaced belts and battery cables, and then precisely adjusted the engine on a scope and analyzer. After paying a good-sized bill, the customer drove off with a smile, obviously satisfied with the work we did.

Fifteen minutes later, he came walking back. His car made it four blocks, quit dead, and wouldn't restart. The poor customer had four long blocks walking back in pouring rain to work up a good, righteous anger.

A quiet young mechanic named Mike took the customer's keys and disappeared. Mike drove the car back a few minutes later, gave the customer his keys and said softly, "Sir, you better fill up with gas before you go too far, all you have now is the gallon I just poured in."

The customer broke off his tirade in mid-gesture and there was a long pause. Then he laughed and said, "You're probably going to tell this story for years." And so I have. But after that, I checked the gas tank on every car before it left my shop!

All technicians make mistakes. Fortunately, most of them are discovered during postrepair testing and corrected at the shop's expense. Once in awhile, a mistake slips past and the car is delivered to the customer who later discovers the problem. If you have this sort of experience, of course you're going to take the car back to the shop that did the work. On your way back, remember that an automobile may have some 10,000 parts and that it's not unheard of for two or more things to act up at the same time. Your mechanic may have diagnosed and corrected one problem that needed fixing but overlooked the second one.

"A good mechanic, working in a good shop, will always correct a mistake at the shop's expense. That's part of the guarantee you can expect from your regular mechanic."
T.K.

47

UNDERSTANDING YOUR CAR

With nearly 10,000 individual parts, it's no wonder most of us feel intimidated at the prospect of learning how a car works. But taken as individual units or systems, such as the cooling system, brakes or suspension, the process becomes much simpler. More important, having a basic understanding of how your car works is essential to keeping it in good health.

Many mechanics compare keeping your car running well with keeping your body in good shape. Both your car and your body warn of impending disaster with innocent early symptoms and both will last longer if treated to regular checkups and kept in good condition.

Like aerobic exercise which helps a human live longer and better, your car also needs to be "exercised" with an occasional freeway run at the speed limit. Stop-and-go driving is the automotive equivalent of a sedentary lifestyle.

Having a regular mechanic who knows you and your automobile is as important to your car as your family practitioner is important to your physical health. When your car develops symptoms, a good mechanic is likely to tell you he needs to perform some tests before he makes a diagnosis.

New automobile technologies always produce new worries among car owners. Today's concern is about computerization.

Many mechanics report that consumers want them "to take out the computer and replace it with a good, old- fashioned electronic ignition!" A few years ago owners were asking, "How much is it to take out this electronic ignition and put in a good, old-fashioned points and condenser?" This phenomenon is certainly not new. When hydraulic brakes were first introduced, some owners wanted the "newfangled" hydraulic brakes removed and replaced with good, old-fashioned mechanical brakes.

Inevitably the introduction of new products brings about new problems. Often these are a function of design defects or assembly problems that are quickly worked out. This is one reason we never recommend buying a car during its first model year of production. Nevertheless, we believe that the new technology in today's cars is, for the most part, good news. The bad news is that these new cars are less able to be serviced by a friendly local garage and one is often required to go back to more expensive dealer shops for repairs.

An economic fact of life is that all cars, new and old, require maintenance—the more you understand about your car the less frustrated and expensive that process will be.

Consider this: Every item you repair or replace an item that's one more item that's as good as new.

"I once bought a 5 year-old compact car for fifty dollars. It had a rebuilt engine, tires like new, a freshly overhauled, transmission, a new radiator and the brakes had less than 1000 miles on them. The car would not start. The owner was thoroughly disgusted and determined to get rid of it because it was "dollaring him to death"— costing him too much in repairs.

I towed it to my shop and replaced a fuel pump interlock switch which cost me about three dollars. The former owner had paid to correct every major wear point, then ran out of patience within three dollars of having a trouble-free car! He did not have an understanding of the whole car as a single machine made up of parts." T.K.

Thermostat: The Cooling System's Gatekeeper

The thermostat in your car's cooling system is an automobile part that has remained unchanged for many years. Many people, including mechanics, never stop to think of the excellent engineering that went into the design of a thermostat. What is remarkable is that in this era of computerized brakes and fuel injection, the design of the thermostat remains untouched.

The thermostat is located in your engine's cooling system and is essentially a valve that opens and closes depending on how hot the coolant in your system is. When the thermostat is closed, the coolant just circulates around the engine. When your engine heats up and the coolant gets hot, the thermostat opens to let the coolant in from the radiator.

Inside the thermostat is a wax pellet. As coolant temperature rises, the pellet begins to expand. Thermal expansion is a powerful force and as the pellet enlarges, it pushes against a spring and the valve begins to open. At the thermostat's rated temperature, it is fully open. The temperature is set at the factory and is accomplished by varying the amount of wax in the pellet. The thermostat usually begins to open about twenty degrees below its rated temperature. It opens and closes as the temperature of the coolant rises and falls which keeps the coolant at a constant temperature.

If your engine overheats regularly, resist the temptation to remove the thermostat. A cold-running engine will dramatically reduce fuel efficiency. Most engines are designed to operate efficiently at 180 degrees. An engine running at 125 degrees can waste one out of every ten gallons of gas. A faulty thermostat can be a major cause of poor fuel economy. If you feel your car should be getting better fuel economy, have your thermostat checked. They are inexpensive and easy to replace.

"A cold-running engine can cause nearly as many problems as one that runs too hot. Replacing your thermostat is an inexpensive, but important preventive maintenance item that's often overlooked." J.G.

51

What Does Horsepower Really Mean?

In the early days of automobiles, drivers could relate to driving a horseless carriage with five or ten horsepower. Today, the thought of controlling a vehicle propelled by the power of 300 horses conjures up quite a different image. Actually, horsepower has little to do with the power of a horse. A strong horse has only about half a horsepower.

Power is the rate at which work is done. Consider this: You could easily lift 33,000 pounds of bricks a distance of one foot. You'd have to lift them one at a time and may take all summer to do it, but you could do it. To raise that 33,000 pounds a distance of one foot in one minute, requires work at the rate of one horsepower.

The horsepower ratings assigned to automobile engines use a measure called SAE (Society of Automotive Engineers) horsepower. It is based on the cylinder bore, the stroke, the number of cylinders, all multiplied by an arbitrary "fudge factor." Just as horsepower has little to do with the power of a horse, the Society of Automotive Engineers had nothing to do with inventing SAE horsepower. The concept was actually originated decades ago by the Royal Automobile Club of England.

Every car on the market today has enough horsepower to get you from point A to point B at legal speeds or faster. If you drive at the speed limit, or within 20 percent of it, excess horsepower merely costs you money because smaller engines generally get better mileage.

Another way to measure an engine's power is by its compression ratio. Your engine's compression is defined by the ratio of the volume inside the cylinder at two different times. The first is when the piston is at the bottom of its stroke, the second when the piston is at the top. For example, if the volume when the

"Another measure of engine size is the total volume inside the cylinder. In the past this was measured in cubic inches. Today's cars are measured in liters. A 2.0 liter engine has larger (or more) cylinders than a 1.8 liter engine, and thus, is more powerful." J.G.

piston is at the bottom is eighty cubic centimeters and ten when it's at the top, then the compression ratio is eight to one. Sometimes this is described as a compression ratio of eight. Generally, lower compression ratios mean less power and higher ratios mean more power.

Over the years, compression ratios have edged upward. The compression ratio chosen by the manufacturer is a tradeoff between operating costs and cooling system efficiency. As the compression ratio goes up, the fuel efficiency improves but the operating temperature increases. Higher compression with its better fuel efficiency meant decreased levels of hydrocarbon (HC) and carbon monoxide (CO) in the exhaust. Unfortunately, those higher temperatures tended to increase the formation of oxides of nitrogen (NOX), the ingredient that made Los Angeles smog famous.

So, manufacturers struck a compromise—a compression ratio that was high enough to reduce HC and CO, but low enough to emit acceptable levels of NOX. Soon, even lower standards were mandated for all three. An impossible problem? Not really, but it required some ingenious solutions. As compressions went higher a catalytic converter was added to "burn" the HC and to convert the CO into harmless carbon dioxide. An exhaust gas recirculation (EGR) valve was also added. The EGR sent some of the exhaust gas back into the engine to be recycled. This reduced the percentage of oxygen, combustion chamber temperatures, and oxides of nitrogen.

Identifying Your Engine

There is some very important information about your engine on a label underneath the hood that may come in handy for a mechanic, even if you never look at it. Before engines became so sophisticated, tuneups for almost every one were identical. Now in order to adjust an engine properly, the mechanic must have the manufacturers' specifications for that particular engine.

The mechanic's first step is to identify the engine. This is no longer a simple task. A single manufacturer in a single model year may install a half dozen different engines, some of which are made by other manufacturers. In order to identify the engine, every car has a rectangular decal under the hood displaying information about the engine, its ignition system, and its emission control system. You will usually find the decal on the inside wall of the fender, the underside of the hood, or attached to the engine on the side of a valve cover. Wherever it is, that decal is important.

First, it is imprinted with the model year and the engine size and type. Because this will be the actual year the manufacturer made the engine, it may be different from what's listed on your title or registration. Second, the decal displays tuneup specifications, sometimes a diagram of your timing segment, a vacuum system diagram, and other useful information. The data and diagrams on your underhood decal are just as meaningful when the car is 10 years old as when the car is new.

If, over a time your decal becomes illegible, you can buy a new one from your car dealer. Because the easiest way to buy the correct replacement is to have the data from the old one, the best time to buy is when the car is new and the decal is easy to read. You can tuck it in your owner's manual and keep it in the glove

"The older you car gets, the more important it is to know exactly what kind of engine you have. Knowing your engine's identification will help ensure that you're getting the right replacement parts." J.G.

box. Another good idea is to write the identity of your engine indelibly inside the owner's manual, and maybe on your title. It can't hurt to be redundant, and it may help.

There are two basic types of engines found in today's cars: gasoline and diesel. Gasoline engines are by far the most popular. The diesel engine, though far less popular, deserves a few words. The diesel engine was invented during the nineteenth century, by Rudolph Diesel and has been used in automobiles for almost sixty years. These engines have some intriguing advantages, the first of which is economy. Customarily, a diesel powered car will get better mileage on less expensive fuels. They run consistently cooler, with combustion chamber temperatures 300 to 500 degrees lower than gasoline engines.

Diesel engines offer high torque (the turning power of the drive shaft) at low speeds, which contributes to economy. They have the disadvantage of being considerably heavier, horsepower for horsepower, than gasoline engines. Diesel engines are sternly unforgiving of fuel contamination, even the tiniest bit of water condensation, and they are more complex, and harder to service than gasoline engines. As diesel engines have become more common, ingenious technology has evolved to simplify formerly tedious service.

Air: Filtering, Turbocharging, and Carbureting

Your car's engine needs air (oxygen) to burn fuel. The air filter and turbocharging systems play important roles in getting air into the engine.

The air filter removes particles from the air that the carburetor mixes with gasoline. Modern air filters are made of specially treated and folded paper held in place between two plastic rings. As air passes through the filter, the sand, grit, metal, and any other particles flying around your engine compartment become trapped in the filter.

As particles collect, the flow is restricted. Too little air is the same as too much fuel, and the engine develops all the symptoms of running rich, including bad mileage.

Some do-it-yourselfers try to tap dirt out of air filters, and some mechanics try to blow dirt out with compressed air. This cannot possibly remove the tiny particles caught in the fibers of the filter paper. To see how clogged your filter is, hold the filter up to a strong light. If you can't see light through it, replace it. In any event, replace your filter at every tuneup, and more often in severely dusty driving conditions.

In order to get more power out of a smaller engine, your car may have a turbocharger. A turbocharger is basically an air pump that forces more air into the engine for combustion. Most turbochargers consist of an air compressor driven by a small turbine wheel powered by the engine's exhaust. Taking advantage of energy otherwise lost, the turbine forces the fuel-air mixture into the cylinders, improving the efficiency of the engine. Turbochargers are often used to increase the power of small engines.

Engines equipped with turbochargers are certainly more expensive than standard engines. The extra power may not be necessary

"If you buy a new car and the standard engine on the model you want doesn't offer enough power, consider a larger standard engine rather than a turbocharged engine. You'll save on repair costs later on." J.G.

when you consider the extra expense and the fact that turbocharging adds to the complexity of the engine and increases repair costs.

A carburetor is the device that mixes air with the gasoline. The mixture varies depending on the needs of the engine. Lean mixtures mean more air, rich mean more gas.

It's often said that seven of every ten cars on the road need carburetor work. The statement may be true, especially if we include idles that need adjustment, defective chokes, bad gaskets, and loose mounting bolts. The complaint that brings many drivers to a repair shop, sometimes on the end of a towing hook, is carburetor flooding.

The most common cause of flooding is a float (the part of the carburetor that literally floats on a reservoir of gas) that has become soggy because it's penetrated by gasoline. Years ago, floats were hollow and made of thin brass. Now they're almost all made of a plastic foam, which is a genuine improvement. The tiniest pinhole in an old brass float meant you were stalled, without warning, wherever it happened. The newer plastic float has thousands of tiny cells. If they fail, it's one at a time, giving the driver plenty of warning.

The plastic would stand up against pure gasoline forever, but starting in the Seventies, as refiners coaxed more gallons of gasoline from each barrel of crude, they began developing new additives. Some of these additives were ferocious solvents and among the things they dissolved were the early plastic floats. New plastic formulas have been developed to withstand all present additives.

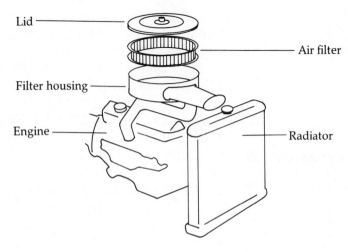

Air Filter

Under the Hood: Wires and Belts

Two of the most prominent items you'll notice when you open your car's hood are spark plug wires and belts. These simple parts are vital to your car's operation. Your car's spark plug wires must be hooked up correctly to insure that each spark plug "fires" in the right order. This is based on your particular engine design and varies from car to car. Cylinders are numbered from the front to the rear of an engine, except for Jaguars which are numbered rear-to-front.

A four cylinder engine most often has a firing order of 1-3-4-2. That means the number one, or front cylinder, fires first; then number three, the third one back. Number four follows, and finally number two. Caution: That is not always the firing order, merely the most common! Other types of engines will have different firing orders and numbering schemes.

It's wise for a do-it-yourselfer to change one spark plug or one spark plug wire at a time, to avoid mixing up the firing order. Unfortunately, if the engine was running badly because some wires were reversed, this method faithfully perpetuates the error. The shop manual for your car and many tuneup manuals will have a diagram showing your car's cylinder numbering scheme, the direction of cylinder rotation, and the location in the distributor cap of the number one plug wire.

An engine that has had the plug wires installed in the wrong order may not run at all. If it does, it can produce spectacular backfiring. If you suspect this problem, be sure you've identified your engine, then consult the diagram. On some engines, the distributor may have been removed, then carelessly replaced in the wrong position. In this event, it's wise to have a professional reposition the distributor.

"Once you think of it as an investment, learning about your car is less of a tedious chore. Even if you don't understand cars, you know the cost and aggravation involved when they don't work." T.K.

58

In addition to spark plug wires you will notice a number of belts. These belts transmit engine power to various other items in the engine compartment. They used to be called fan belts when all they drove was the fan. Today, they are called drive or V (because of their shape) belts. A number of factors determine how long they will last. If pulleys they run on are out of line, belts can wear and fray pretty fast. If they are too loose, they can slip, causing over-heating and premature cracking. If the belt is too tight, fibers can be stretched, and the belt can crack. An oil leak that drips on the belt will soften it, dramatically shortening its expected life.

But the right size and contour belt, correctly installed and ten-sioned on properly functioning equipment, should last many thousands of miles. If a mechanic says you need new belts, ask him to show you why. It's often a sign of another problem.

One last note of common sense: If your car has more than one belt and you replace one, replace them all at the same time. Murphy's Law says that the next one to fail will be the innermost, hardest to reach, and most expensive to change.

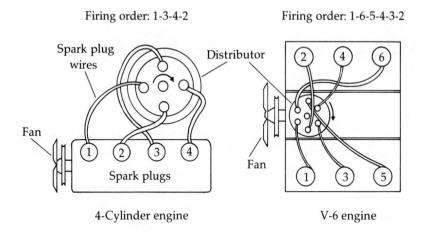

Firing order: 1-3-4-2   Firing order: 1-6-5-4-3-2

4-Cylinder engine   V-6 engine

Spark Plug Wires: Typical Configurations

Some Disclosures About Distributors

The distributor sends electricity to the spark plugs in the exact order they need to fire at just the right time. Inside the distributor a rotating cam makes electrical contact with a set of metal "points." Each time the cam passes one of the points, an electrical charge is sent to the ignition coil where the voltage is greatly increased. This charge is then routed to the spark plugs via the spark plug wires. Today, these mechanical distributors are being replaced by solid-state distributors with no moving parts.

Even though mechanical distributors may be on the way out, there are millions still on the road and millions still being manufactured. There's a crucial fact about mechanical distributors that a large number of mechanics fail to realize. The gap between the tip of the revolving rotor and the stationary electrodes arranged around the inside of the cap is very specific. The dimension of that gap is critical. With electronic ignition, and the even more precise computerized ignition, the size of that distributor gap has become crucial. The only way to set the gap inside the distributor is to replace both the rotor and cap at the same time.

There's little doubt mechanical distributors will linger awhile because there are so many in use. But when the last mechanical distributor is towed to a recycling yard a lot of problems will go with it. The solid-state distributor, as its name suggests, has no moving parts. The earlier electronic distributors got rid of only part of the problem. With them, away went "points bounce," inertia, corrosion, and wear at the points. But even with the electronic distributor, we still had a rotating shaft, a rotor, and a cap with terminals and all their associated problems.

The solid state distributor eliminates all those problems, because it has no shaft, no

"At tuneup time, whether you do-it-yourself or have a shop do it for you, replacing the rotor without replacing the cap is like trying to applaud with one hand." T.K.

rotor, and no cap. It uses external sensing to determine which spark plugs to fire.

Mechanical distributors are still with us, however, and almost every one has a distributor advance unit. Let's examine how the unit functions. When you step on the gas pedal to call for more power from the engine, your carburetor allows more fuel-air mixture into the cylinders. Each cylinder needs more time to burn this mixture fully, so the spark plug must fire earlier in the compression stroke. The advance unit, which is mounted on the side of the distributor, senses vacuum from the carburetor. The vacuum pulls a diaphragm that causes your timing to advance. If the vacuum line becomes plugged or broken, or the diaphragm punctures or gets stuck, the timing can't advance. Here's what you'll notice from the driver's seat: When you step on the gas pedal to pull away from a stop, the engine will hesitate, backfire, or stall. The car will be sluggish and your mileage will drop off suddenly and noticeably.

If you ever meet this combination of symptoms, ask your mechanic to test your advance unit, and be sure it's checked at every tuneup. Replacing a defective distributor advance unit will stop the backfiring, improve the bad mileage, and restore the lost power. Dollar for dollar, it's one of the most productive repairs that can be made on a car.

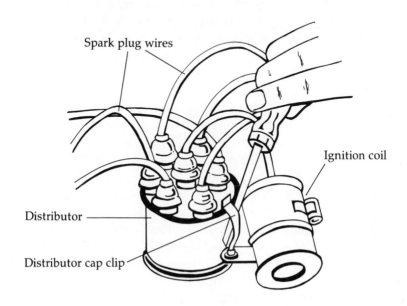

Spark plug wires

Ignition coil

Distributor

Distributor cap clip

A Typical Distributor

Automatic Action: Transmissions and Chokes

The most underserviced part of your car is likely to be your automatic transmission. One reason is because it is a virtually sealed unit, inherently clean, and highly reliable. Transmission fluid does not wear out or become contaminated with acids, as engine oil does. A properly adjusted transmission with a working filter and regularly changed transmission fluid could theoretically last forever.

But every year some twelve million automatic transmissions wear out or need to be rebuilt. About 90 percent of that damage is done by heat. Heat causes the transmission fluid to break down and begin the telltale change in color. Once that starts, clutch materials begin to erode and before long the transmission is a piece of expensive junk.

You could burn up the fluid in a new transmission within 200 or so miles by towing an overload up a hill on a hot day. You can guard against such damage by making sure the fluid in your automatic transmission is filled. There is a dipstick located under your hood which will tell you your fluid level. If your car owner's manual doesn't show you, your regular mechanic can teach you in about thirty seconds where the dipstick is located. With the engine running and the selector in park, check your fluid at least four times a year or every 100 miles if you're towing something or if your driving conditions are exceptionally hilly. Learn to recognize the bright red color and healthy aroma of clean transmission fluid. You should have the transmission serviced and adjusted if you detect the slightest tinge of brown (or any color other than bright red) or the tiniest hint of a burned smell. You'll also need a new filter and pan gasket.

If you do a lot of severe driving, consider having an auxiliary transmission fluid cooler

"Compared to the cost of a new transmission, regular service and inspection is trivial." J.G.

"The square wheel wasn't really that great an idea. Neither was the hand choke!" T.K.

installed. This device can extend the life of your transmission for tens of thousands of miles. The cooler mounts in front of your radiator and the automatic transmission fluid is circulated through it. It's important to install a cooler that's large enough. This will depend on the size of your engine and the load you carry, and also on the kind of driving you do. Tip: It's better to install a cooler that's too big than one that's too small. Check the installation for leaks during the first few thousand miles.

Another automatic device on your car is the choke. Every mechanic who ever twisted a wrench has heard customers say, "My automatic choke is not working right, please take it out and install a good, old-fashioned hand choke."

Comparing hand chokes with automatic chokes is like comparing a square wheel with a round one. The square wheel, or skid, did lend itself to a certain amount of refinement. But no matter how much the skid was improved, it was doomed to obsolescence once the concept of the round wheel was introduced. The old hand choke was refined over the years, but it can't hold a candle to a properly functioning automatic choke.

Things *can* go wrong with an automatic choke. The choke thermostat can fail or fall out of adjustment, especially if a vehicle moves from one climate or altitude to another. The vacuum pulloff unit can be defective or out of adjustment. Every automatic choke requires the use of some kind of cold idle adjustment, usually a setscrew riding on a cam. On some cars, cold idle setting is accomplished with an electric solenoid, which itself can fail or fall victim to a bad wire.

If your automatic choke misbehaves, don't replace it with a hand choke kit. Instead, have the automatic choke serviced and all its functions checked out by a trained technician.

Power: Steering and Brakes

Once a luxury, most cars today come with power steering and power brakes. Understanding how they work will help you avoid expensive repairs. There are four major manufacturers of automotive power steering units, and they all get the same job done. Power steering works because a hydraulic pump takes a small amount of power from the engine, then directs the resulting hydraulic pressure to an actuating cylinder that reinforces the direction you are turning the wheel and helps out. It uses the engine power to help you steer.

Keeping the power steering reservoir filled with the proper type of fluid is the easiest thing you can do to maintain this system. The reservoir is usually located in the engine compartment near the steering wheel. Consult your owner's manual or mechanic for the exact location.

The power steering pump is driven by a *V* belt. The belt should be inspected regularly, and replaced at the slightest sign of wear. If you've ever tried to turn your wheels with the engine off, you have an idea what could happen if the belt broke at freeway speed.

Belt tension is important. If it's too loose, power will not be transmitted to the pump because the belt will slip. Slipping causes the belt to wear prematurely. If the tension is too tight, you risk damaging the pump bearings.

If your power steering becomes noisy, that usually means fluid is low and there are air bubbles in the system. First, top off with the proper fluid and then, with the engine running, turn the steering wheel full left to full right several times. That should quiet things down.

Disc and drum brakes are genuine marvels of modern technology. Yet they work on an ancient principle discovered by a Greek named Archimedes a couple of thousand years before the automobile was invented: Pressure applied to any part of a closed fluid system is transmitted equally to all parts of the system. That means you can step on the brake pedal in your driver's compartment, and pressure is applied equally to the brakes at all four wheels.

The only requirement is that your brakes be part of a *closed* system, which means no leaks. Generally, fluid brakes are quite reliable and long-lasting, but leaks which allow fluid to seep out or air to leak in, can develop. Check your brake fluid level at the master cylinder once in awhile (you can locate this under the hood easily enough yourself or have your mechanic do it), to protect against low fluid. If air gets into a line, brakes will feel spongy and you should have them checked by a professional.

Brake fluid attracts water from vapor in the atmosphere and it should be flushed out and replaced every few years, to prevent the water from rusting the steel tubing or pitting the wheel cylinders. A certified brake technician will do this every time he changes your pads or linings.

If your car has power brakes, they use a vacuum system to amplify the pressure you apply to the brake pedal. Under the hood and directly in front of the brake pedal, you'll find the vacuum diaphragm housing. Depending on the car, this will be eight to fourteen inches in diameter, and three to five inches thick. Inside are two chambers, separated by a rugged, durable diaphragm. The center of the diaphragm is connected to the rod linking the brake pedal to the master cylinder. There's a hose, about the diameter of your thumb, running from the forward end of the diaphragm housing to the intake manifold of the engine, where it picks up vacuum.

When you have power brakes only part of the energy that stops the car comes directly from your foot. As the pedal moves, it opens a valve that allows pressure to push on the diaphragm. The amount of pressure is controlled by your foot movement, and it is considerable. The pressure pushes the linkage rod in the same direction as your foot movement, thereby "boosting" your effort, and slowing or stopping the car with little exertion on your part.

Since the vacuum comes from the intake manifold, power brakes will not provide boost unless the engine is running, though there is often a vacuum reservoir that will provide enough reserve for one or two stops. Driving a car with disabled power brakes can be dangerous, because the effort required to slow or stop is many times more than what you are used to.

Your Emission Control System

Emission control in its early days picked up a bad reputation because many mechanics had not learned to service the unfamiliar systems. Worse yet, different manufacturers used, and still use, different approaches and the mechanic had to learn not one, but a dozen different emission control systems (ECS). With today's emphasis on mechanic training, it's not nearly such a big problem.

Many elements of your ECS actually improve your mileage. A vapor recovery canister, for example, captures gasoline fumes from the gas tank and carburetor fuel bowl, condenses the fumes back into liquid gasoline and re-injects the gasoline into your engine. Even so, many owners cut and plug the lines to their vapor recovery canisters because they mistakenly believe they will get better mileage.

Your regular mechanic can test your emission control system and keep it serviced. When it's working right, you'll hardly know it's there. Tampering with it is illegal.

Among the most primitive of emission devices is the positive crankcase ventilation (PCV) valve. It's been around for so long you'd think all mechanics would be aware of its service needs. But that's not the case. A few mechanics still use the old "shake it and if it rattles it's okay" test on PCV valves. This is not to be trusted. Too many gummed-up PCV valves rattle just fine when shaken, but promptly stick when re-installed.

PCV valves are inexpensive and should be replaced at every tuneup. At the same time, you should replace the breather filter. A new one is about two dollars and well worth it in improved mileage and longer engine life. It will take your mechanic about fifteen seconds to install one.

The catalytic converter is a device in the

"I had a standard answer when a customer asked me how much I'd charge to remove his emission control system. $10,050. That was fifty dollars to do the work and $10,000 to pay the fine. Many owners mistakenly believe that the "pollution junk" on a car reduces their mileage. The fact is, a properly functioning emission control system has an insignificant effect on your mileage." T.K.

exhaust system that looks like a small, flat muffler. As its name suggests, it contains a catalyst, platinum, and it converts harmful exhaust ingredients into harmless products. It accomplishes this by encouraging burning, or oxidation, of residual hydrocarbons (HC) and carbon monoxide (CO). The hydrocarbons become water (H_2O) and carbon dioxide (CO_2). The poisonous carbon monoxide becomes carbon dioxide, the same gas that makes bubbles in your soft drink.

Because they reduce HC and CO emissions, catalytic converters deceived early exhaust gas analyzers and concealed engine malfunctions such as misfiring or rich mixture. This led to the development of new analyzers. These are called "four-gas" analyzers because they monitor the exhaust for carbon monoxide, carbon dioxide, hydrocarbons, and oxygen. From these readings, a technician can tell the difference between engine problems and converter malfunctions.

Expected life of a catalytic converter is around 50,000 miles or five years. (The government requires that they be guaranteed for that long in new cars.) Use of leaded gasoline or prolonged rich running can drastically reduce that life. A plugged converter can cause serious loss of engine power and poor gas mileage. If your car is nearing 5 years or 50,000 miles, it's a good idea to have your exhaust checked on a four-gas analyzer.

There is a temptation, especially among misinformed automotive hobbyists, to remove catalytic converters and replace them with straight-through "test pipes." In addition to being illegal, there's now conclusive proof this procedure leads to loss of power and excessive engine wear. If you bought your car used, you may want to check to make sure the catalytic converter is intact. Your car needs it.

One of the causes of pollution is incompletely burned gasoline. The fuel in an engine has only a split second to burn on each power stroke. Inevitably, incompletely burned gasoline finds its way into the exhaust causing pollution. One of the devices devised to combat the problem is known as the air injector reactor. This system has been around for over twenty years. One part of the system, its air pump, picked up the nickname of "smog pump." This is an ironic misnomer, since the air injection reactor pumps nothing but clean, fresh air.

The fresh air is pumped or "injected" into the exhaust immediately after the very hot but incompletely burned mixture exits the cylinders. There it completes the combustion of any unburned gasoline and also helps turn poisonous carbon monoxide into harmless carbon dioxide.

The idea is simple, but a few things can go wrong. If the pump stops working, your mileage may go down and you could ruin the drive belt that makes it go. Another more insidious problem occurs when the combustion in the exhaust manifold (the large pipes coming right off the engine) makes a sound that's easy to confuse with bearing noise or pinging. Bearing noise, especially on a low-mileage car, is easy to rule out. The pinging, on the other hand, can cause a mechanic problems. The classic cure for pinging is to retard the timing a little. Unfortunately, this remedy would make air knock worse!

Here's the right way for your mechanic to test for exhaust manifold knock: Drive the car under conditions that produce the sound. Then remove the belt that drives the air pump and drive the car the same way. If the noise goes away, it's a safe bet it was in the exhaust manifold. Caution: On many cars, the same belt that drives the air pump also drives the water pump, so the car shouldn't be driven too far or the engine will overheat.

To treat the condition, just be sure timing is set properly, all advance devices are working, and all tuneup parts are okay. Use the gasoline recommended for the engine. After that, learn to accept the noise. When you know what it is, it won't sound so loud.

Your Fuel Filter Can Let You Down

Most drivers of diesel cars are aware of the importance of regular fuel filter service because diesels are so sensitive to contaminated fuel. But drivers of gasoline cars too frequently put fuel filters in the "drive it until it breaks" category. This can be especially harmful if you drive a fuel-injected car where clean fuel is a must.

The job of the fuel filter is to remove any dirt or contamination from the gas before it reaches the sensitive carburetor or fuel injection components. Of course, the longer it does its job, the less it is able to function properly because the material it traps will eventually clog up the filter. When this happens the engine won't run, or will run so poorly the car will scarcely move. The fuel filter should be changed at every tuneup, and that means at least every 12,000 miles.

At one time, there was just one type of fuel filter. Now there are dozens of different styles, some with two hose connections, some with three, some with none. It would be wise to buy the exact replacement for your car and know how to change it. Then if you're far from home, it's late and all the shops and stores are closed, you can change your fuel filter if your car develops symptoms of fuel starvation, and be glad you prepared in advance.

Fuel filter

Carburetor

Fuel Filter

Take Care of Your Tires

Many drivers do not "rotate" their tires, because they've heard that radial tires should not be rotated. That's a partial truth, that can cost about 20 percent of the mileage that's engineered into your new tires!

Unlike the old bias-ply tires, which were rotated in a criss-cross pattern, radial tires should only be rotated from front-to-rear on the same side of the car. Because steering happens in front, the geometry more complex and alignment more fragile, front tires wear faster and more unevenly than rears. This wear is compounded with front wheel drive cars.

Rotation should be done every 5,000 miles. Some tire stores offer free lifetime rotation if you buy tires from them, and it never hurts to ask. A professional shop can lift all four wheels off the ground and rotate tires in a few minutes, for just a few dollars. They'll know the proper rotation pattern, and they'll inspect the tires as they do the work.

You can do this comparatively simple job yourself. Back off each lug nut about a quarter-turn before you jack up the car. You'll need at least two safety jack stands, and four will make the job go faster. You can rent them or buy them at an auto parts store. Remember to be extra careful when using a bumper jack. Follow the rotation in your shop manual, or ask your tire dealer.

If you have to replace tires, there is generally no problem mixing brands. Just be sure the size of old and new tires match exactly. Never mix types of tires. Problems arise because bias and radial tires differ in their handling characteristics. They change shape differently as they roll. When replacing one tire of a set, it's best to replace it with the identical size and type as the other three.

"By rotating your tires every 5,000 miles, you can get an extra 10,000 miles of safe tire life." T.K.

Wheel balancing can improve your car's handling and safety. Balancing would never be necessary if tires could be manufactured to be perfectly round and with uniform density. In addition, a tire does not wear evenly. As it wears, it tends to go out of balance.

Wheels are balanced by installing small lead weights. While these are strong and reliable, a wheel may occasionally lose a weight and go out of balance. It's wise to have wheel balance checked any time you notice vibration at the steering wheel, or any time you notice uneven tire wear, especially "cupping," which means the tread wears in a cup shape from the size of a quarter to the size of a softball.

Another good time to check wheel balance is before leaving to go on a long trip. In the process of balancing, the shop has the opportunity to inspect tires for cuts, embedded nails, and pieces of glass. Modern electronic balancing machines are speedy and precise, and the process is not expensive. In addition to producing a smoother ride, driving with balanced wheels extends the life of your tires and reduces wear on wheel bearings and suspension parts. It saves you money, improves your comfort, and increases your safety.

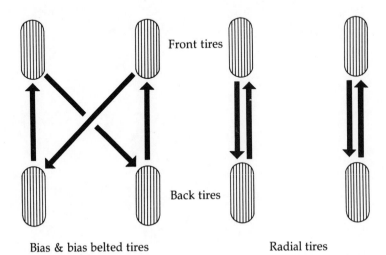

Front tires

Back tires

Bias & bias belted tires   Radial tires

Tire Rotation

KEEPING IT GOING

A few years ago the phrase "fill it up and check the oil" was so common that it seemed like one word. Today, with the popularity of self-service gasoline stations, many of us overlook checking those items that can prevent serious problems down the road.

Here are some tips and techniques for keeping your car out of the shop in the first place. Many of these service checks are ones you can make yourself. Spending fifteen minutes a month on maintenance and making some adjustments in your driving techniques can decrease the likelihood of a major problem later on.

After the initial purchase, car repairs are one of the most expensive aspects of owning an automobile. Because preventive maintenance (PM) items are often a big component of those costs, we tend to avoid them. Many of us take the attitude, "if it isn't broken, don't fix it." Most mechanics will tell you that most of the major and expensive repairs they do are a result of a car owner failing to do basic PM or not responding to a warning signal. That's why we've included this section—to give you some tried and true and little-known tips for *keeping it going*.

Probably the most important tool for keeping your car going is the most overlooked—your owner's manual. Once we've figured out all the gadgets on the dashboard, most of us completely ignore the owners manual. That's a mistake for two reasons. First, to make sure your warranty remains in force, it's important to review the manufacturer recommendations in the book. Second, your owner's manual can lead you to key checks that are easy even for the non-mechanic. For example, checking the brake, power steering and water reservoirs is easier than ever because most manufacturers have made them out of opaque plastic with special refill marks.

There is no reason why, with proper maintenance, a car shouldn't last at least 100,000 miles. In addition, the longer you keep your car, the less expensive it will be to operate. In a study of automobile operating costs, Hertz determined that keeping a car for ten years instead of five will reduce your expenses by one-third. If that's not reason enough to take good care of this expensive purchase, consider this: During the last ten years the median price of a new car has nearly doubled! Imagine what a 1999 model will cost!

Keeping it going means not breaking down. The two most common causes of breakdowns are running out of gas and having a flat tire. To prevent running out of gas, develop the habit of driving off the top half of your tank. When the needle falls to halfway, fill up.

With a flat tire, advance preparation is your best friend. We recommend practicing a tire change in the safety of your own driveway. That's when you'll know where everything is and exactly how to do it in the event of a flood. Those two bits of preparation, driving off the top half of the tank and practicing a tire change, will protect you against the two most common breakdown emergencies. Read on for some other tips.

"Most of us avoid regular PM because we don't like the idea of paying a mechanic $50-100 per year to conduct some tests and checks when there is no apparent problem. Consider this: Instead of gambling with the purchase of an expensive service contract, invest $50-100 in regular PM checks. You'll save on the cost of the service contract (which is of dubious value) and dramatically reduce expensive repairs because you failed to note an important warning signal." J.G.

Oil: Your Car's Lifeblood

Most of us know that an engine's oil is a vital lubricant, but did you know that it provides almost half an engine's cooling? In addition, although running a small, high RPM engine two quarts low on oil may never cause the oil pressure warning light to go on, it may still cut the life of the engine in half! That's why checking your oil is so important. And with the advent of self-service gas stations, we can no longer depend on gas station attendants to do the job.

To check your oil, first turn off the engine. Find the dipstick. Look for a loop made of flat wire located on the side of the engine. If the engine has been running, be careful because the dipstick and surrounding engine parts will be hot. Grab the loop, pull out the dipstick, wipe it off and reinsert it into the engine. Pull it out again and observe the oil level. You can see that *full* and *add* are marked at the end of the stick. If the level is between *add* and *full* you are okay. If it is below, you should add oil until it reaches the *full* line. To put in the oil, remove the cap at the top of the engine. You may have to add more than one quart. Get into the habit of checking the oil every 1,000 miles.

Regularly changing your oil is the single most important thing you can do to protect your engine. Your owner's manual should indicate how often the oil needs to be changed. Although the recommended frequency varies somewhat, if you change oil every 3,500 miles, you'll be doing your car a favor. Many owner's manuals also contain instructions for changing the oil and filter. *You should change the oil filter whenever you change the oil.*

The important things about a motor oil are its viscosity and its service grade. Oils are classified first by *viscosity*, which has to do with the size of the opening they will flow through at a

"After using the same brand of oil for five years, a customer came into the shop concerned because in a recent trip he added a quart of another brand. Should he have been concerned? Not a bit, as long as the letters and numbers match, you'll be just fine." T.K.

"When having your oil changed, remind your mechanic about the type of oil your manual recommends." J.G.

standard temperature. The higher the number, the thicker the oil. If you compare SAE 40 oil with SAE 20, you'll find the SAE 40 will not flow as easily. The term SAE 40 is often shortened to the expression 40 weight.

There are also multi-grade oils, the most common of which is 10W-40. The W stands for winter grade. W oils are thinner than the same number without the W so that they flow more easily at winter temperatures. Oil designated 10W-40 contains additives that allow it to flow like a thin 10W oil, yet maintain its ability to form a lubricating film at higher temperatures, like a 40 weight. There are other multi-grades, including 5W-30 and 15W-40. Your owner's manual will tell you exactly what kind of oil you should use to preserve your warranty.

Oil is also classified by *service grades,* such as SE, SF, SF/CC or SF/CD. These are designated by the American Petroleum Institute (API) and indicate the additives present in the oil. Your owner's manual lists the correct oil for your engine by SAE viscosity and API service grade. Remember viscosity or service grade has nothing to do with quality or price! If a label matches your engine's requirements, it's the right oil for your car.

If your dealer or owner's manual recommends 10W-40 oil, service SF, that's the kind to use. There are over 30 national and regional brands that will fit the bill perfectly fine, even if you mix brands. Using the right oil will extend engine life. Using the wrong oil can void your warranty. New engines generally use a lighter motor oil for improved mileage and reduced engine deposits. When having your oil changed, remind your mechanic about the type of oil your manual recommends.

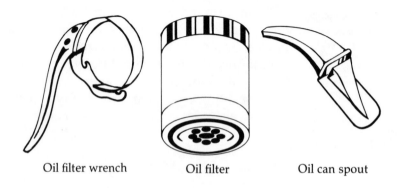

Oil filter wrench   Oil filter   Oil can spout

Changing Your Oil

Transmissions: Preventing an Expensive Repair

An automatic transmission is a complicated assembly and very expensive to replace. Checking your transmission fluid level can prevent an expensive repair job and is easy to do.

First you will have to find the transmission fluid dipstick, just like you'd do to check your oil. It is usually at the rear of the engine and looks like a smaller version of the oil dipstick. To get an accurate reading the engine should be warmed up and running. If the fluid is below the *add* line, add one pint at a time and be sure not to overfill the reservoir. While you are checking the fluid, note its color. It should be a bright, cherry red. If it is a darker, reddish brown the fluid needs changing. If it is very dark, nearly black, and has a burnt smell (like varnish), your transmission may be damaged. Take it to a specialist.

Automatic transmission fluid (ATF) is available at most parts stores. Check your owner's manual for the correct type of fluid for your car. There are two types available. Dextron II and Type F. The difference is subtle, and has to do with viscosity, additives, and slipperiness. Type F has slightly more "bite."

There are two types of clutch materials in automatic transmissions. As time has passed, the quality and tolerances of both clutch materials and both fluid types have improved. Today, each transmission will operate with the wrong kind of fluid. Use the type of automatic transmission fluid recommended by your car's manufacturer, but don't panic if you accidentally add a can of the other type.

"Thousands of automatic transmissions are ruined each year simply because they are driven while low on transmission fluid. With transmission repair as costly as it is, checking your transmission fluid is a money saver." T.K.

77

One of the easiest fluids to check is also one of the most overlooked. Most new cars have a plastic reservoir next to the radiator. This plastic bottle has *full hot* and *full cold* marks on it. If the coolant is below the *full cold* mark, add enough water to bring it up to that mark. Note: If the car is hot, do not open the radiator cap. The pressure and heat that can be released could cause a severe burn.

In most parts of the country a fifty-fifty mixture of antifreeze and water offers adequate protection against freezing. Very cold climates may require more antifreeze. Even if you live where there is no danger of freezing, using the fifty-fifty mixture will keep your cooling system in top shape.

Although it is often labeled "permanent", antifreeze is not permanent in the sense that one fill up will last for the life of your car. The original automotive antifreezes were alcohol based. They kept the cooling systems from freezing, but the boiling point of the alcohol was *lower* than that of water, and a driver had to test and replenish the alcohol supply frequently, or lose the antifreeze protection.

Modern coolants, whatever their color or brand name, are based on ethylene glycol. Pure ethylene glycol remains unfrozen to nine degrees below zero Fahrenheit. As you add water, which freezes at thirty-two degrees *above* zero, an amazing thing happens. The freezing point of the *mixture* goes lower, until a blend of two-thirds ethylene glycol and one-third water won't freeze until ninety-two degrees below zero! For most cars, a fifty-fifty mixture is satisfactory, providing protection to minus thirty-four degrees, or sixty-six degrees below freezing.

At the same time that ethylene glycol lowers the freezing point, it *raises* the boiling point.

A fifty-fifty mixture, used with a standard fifteen-pound pressure cap, won't boil below 265 degrees, compared to 212 degrees for water alone. That's why antifreeze is necessary in the summer as well.

Engine coolants contain rust-, corrosion-, and electrolysis-inhibitors, plus a water pump lubricant. In time, the inhibitors become depleted, as the result of doing their job. Rust from the engine block, minerals from the water and solder from the radiator all contaminate the coolant. So, every other year, the cooling system should be drained, flushed, and refilled with a fifty-fifty mixture of new coolant and water. If you do this yourself, don't let the old coolant drain out onto the ground. Ethylene glycol has a sweet taste, but it's toxic to dogs, cats, and small children.

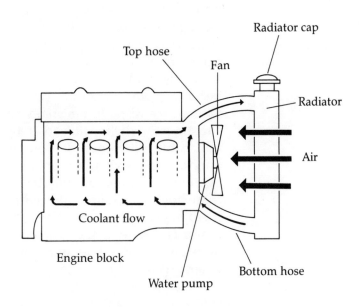

Engine Cooling System

Gas Up Right and Keep the Lead Out

It is illegal to put leaded gasoline into a car labeled unleaded only. But it often happens because the owner is unaware of the consequences. Using leaded gas in an unleaded-gas-only car can ruin the catalytic converter and oxygen sensor, two expensive repair items, in less than 5000 miles.

Trying to save money by using leaded gasoline will cost you in the long run. Misfueling your car can cost you up to nineteen cents per gallon in increased maintenance costs.

Some drivers believe that lead adds power to gasoline. It's not true. The only purpose of lead is to inhibit the knock, or pinging, caused by fuel that is burning unevenly. Newer unleaded gasolines have different, non-polluting additives that reduce pinging and increase the octane rating.

Buying leaded gasoline for older cars will become more difficult as refineries begin to meet new anti-pollution standards. Most consumers can switch to unleaded regular with no noticeable difference. If you notice engine knock, then switch to premium unleaded. Switching to premium will be less expensive than buying gasoline additives and putting them in your tank every time you fill up.

You can save at the gas pump by buying non-branded gasoline and still get the same quality as brand name gasoline. A recent lawsuit allows the nearly 55,000 franchised service stations to sell any brand of gasoline, even if the sign out front names a particular brand. Major oil companies often swap fuel to save on transportation costs, so gasoline sold from a name brand station could have actually come from a competing refiner. When this happens, the company whose name is on the *pump* has the responsibility to put in the advertized additives for that brand.

"When filling up at the gas pump, avoid inhaling gasoline fumes, they are suspected carcinogens. If the fumes are strong enough to smell, change your position to the 'upwind' side." J.G.

Using self-service gas stations also pays off. The average price of a gallon of gasoline is 20 percent less at a self service station. In some areas you can cut your car's gas bill by up to 67 percent. Remember, if you use a self-service station on a regular basis, you need to conduct your own preventive maintenance checks for such items as oil and other fluids.

You have probably noticed that many of the oil companies are actively promoting detergent gasolines. The reason: The high repair bills associated with sophisticated fuel injection systems have been attributed to clogged fuel injectors caused by gasoline. Adding detergent agents to gasoline can reduce clogging and save expensive repair bills.

Most auto manufacturers are strongly recommending the use of detergent gasolines with their fuel injected cars. If you need a detergent gasoline, it pays to shop around. Some oil companies offer detergents only in their premium unleaded gasoline which often costs fifteen cents a gallon more than regular. Other oil companies offer detergents in all grades of gasoline. By using a non-premium grade of detergent gasoline, you can save over $100 per year. Remember: Detergent gasolines are not necessary for cars with standard carburetors.

Here are some tips for improving your mileage: Keep unnecessary weight from accumulating in your car and trunk. Keep your engine tuned. Have your well-maintained emission control system inspected. Keep your tires fully inflated.

Another way to conserve is to anticipate the stop. Take your foot off the pedal early and coast before you brake. Another step you might take is to ask your mechanic to "lean" your accelerator pump. It's a simple task that will gain you some mileage, but you'll be forced to learn to accelerate more slowly, or your engine will stumble.

Checking Your MPG

Checking your gas mileage is a good way to keep tabs on your operating expenses and monitor your engine's health. An increase in fuel consumption can signal a problem, *before* it becomes an expensive repair.

Here's what to do:

• Start with a full tank of gas and note the odometer reading.

• When your tank is nearly empty, fill it up completely and write down the odometer reading and the number of gallons you buy.

• Subtract the first odometer reading from the second and divide your answer by the number of gallons of gas you bought. This is your miles per gallon (MPG).

You will get the best estimate of your car's gas mileage by keeping a record over several tankfuls. There may be a small difference each time because of changes in weather, where you drive, the car's condition, and whether your driving was primarily city or highway.

Warning: Never carry gasoline in a can anywhere in your car. It's at least as dangerous as dynamite. Carry your spare fuel reserve in the bottom half of your gas tank and drive off the top half.

If you have trouble developing economical driving habits, you may want to consider buying a vacuum gauge. This gauge is mounted on your dashboard and has a dial that usually reads *Power Range, Cruising Range,* and *Economy Range.* A needle moves in response to the pressure of your foot on the gas pedal. When you stomp on the gas, the manifold vacuum drops and the needle moves into the red *Power Range.* This means your engine hungrily is devouring fuel. By keeping the needle in the *Economy* or *Cruising Range* you will save gas. A vacuum gauge can be installed by a mechanic relatively inexpensively.

"It may be hard for you to believe that changing your driving habits can double your mileage—but I've have known it to happen!" T.K.

Octane Ratings: What Do They Mean?

The octane rating of a gasoline is not a measure of power or quality. It is simply a measure of the gas's resistance to engine knock. Engine knock is the "pinging" sound you hear when the fuel-air mixture in your engine ignites prematurely during acceleration.

The octane rating appears on a yellow label on the gas pump. Octane ratings vary with the different types of gas (premium or regular), in different parts of the country (higher altitudes require lower octane ratings), and even between brands (Texaco's gasolines may have a different rating than Exxon's).

Most new cars are designed to run on a posted octane rating of 87. This number is the average derived from testing the gasoline under two different conditions. Using the lowest rated gasoline possible will save you money at the fuel pump. Here's how to select the right octane level for your car:

• First, have your engine tuned to exact factory specifications by a competent mechanic and make sure it is in good working condition.

• Next, when the gas in your tank is very low, fill up with the gasoline you usually use. After you have driven ten to fifteen miles, come to a complete stop and accelerate rapidly. If your engine knocks (that pinging sound) during acceleration, you should switch to a higher octane rating. If there is no knocking sound, wait until your tank is very low and fill up with a lower rated gasoline. Then repeat the test. When you reach the level of octane that causes your engine to knock during the test, go back to the next highest rating.

Note: Your engine may knock when you are accelerating a heavily loaded car up a hill or sometimes when the humidity is low. This is normal and generally does not mean you need a higher-octane gas.

Finding the right octane level may also involve blending your own. Try a blend of one gallon of premium fuel for each gallon of regular you put in your tank. You want to find the most economical mixture that allows you to drive with only rare pinging. Another step you can take is to ask your mechanic to retard your timing a degree or two. You may lose 3 percent on your miles per gallon, but you may save 25 percent on the gas you buy.

Gasoline Alternatives

Adding methanol to gasoline is one way to reduce the cost of fuel. However, this practice is not without controversy. In fact, some car manufacturers specifically warn against using gasoline that contains methanol. They claim that adding methanol will cause poorer driveability, deterioration of fuel system parts and poorer fuel economy. Other manufacturers indicate that a certain percentage (generally not more than 5 percent) of methanol will not affect your engine. Those companies that specifically warn against the use of methanol may not cover the cost of certain warranty repairs if methanol is used.

Tip: Since most states do not require gas pumps to display methanol content, ask the service station manager if there is any (and at what percent) in the gasoline you use. Check your owner's manual and warranty before using gasoline with methanol additives.

Another alternative to gasoline is ethyl alcohol. Typically, a mechanic can convert your car to run on pure ethanol in about an hour, for less than $100. However, alcohol is not generally available or widely used in the United States as a motor fuel. The existence of few alcohol-burning cars means that there is small demand for the fuel. We do not recommend conversion until the availability of alcohol fuels increases. There are some technological problems as well. Alcohol is hygroscopic, which means it tends to absorb water vapor from the air. Water dissolved in alcohol can rust steel gas tanks.

If you do use an alcohol blend gasoline, check your fuel filter regularly because alcohol blends tend to clean dirt, rust and grime from the fuel system which will eventually clog the fuel filter. A clogged fuel filter can cause stalling or difficultly in starting a car.

"In Brasil and Peru, automobiles that burn ethyl alcohol are the only ones allowed. Familiar makes are marketed, like Ford, Chevrolet, Chrysler, Volkswagen, Honda. This can be accomplished in the United States only with strong congressional leadership. Ethanol can be made from grain, sugar, fruit, even farm product scraps. Reducing petroleum imports would improve balance of trade. Clean-burning alcohol would eliminate virtually all pollution." T.K.

Brakes, Belts, Steering and Keeping Cool

Your brakes are the most important safety item on the car, yet they are often the most ignored.

Here is a simple test that can signal potential problems with your brakes. If you have power brakes, you will need to have the engine on to do the test. Push the brake pedal down and hold it down. The pedal should stop firmly about halfway to the floor and stay there. If the stop is mushy or the pedal keeps moving slowly to the floor, you should have your brakes checked. Checking the brake fluid on most new cars is very easy. Your owner's manual tells you where the fluid reservoir is located. The reservoir indicates minimum and maximum fluid levels. If you add your own brake fluid, buy it in small cans and keep them tightly sealed. Brake fluid absorbs moisture and excess moisture can damage your brake system. Have your brakes checked if you must regularly replace the brake fluid.

A simple loose belt in the engine can be the cause of electrical problems, cooling problems, even air conditioning problems. You may have one or more belts connected to your engine. To check them, simply push down on the middle of each. It should feel tight. If you can push down more than half an inch, have the belts tightened.

If your car has power steering, find the power steering fluid reservoir when you check your brake fluid. This reservoir is usually behind the steering wheel and connected by a belt to the engine. To check the fluid, simply unscrew the cap and look in the reservoir which usually has markings inside. Some cars have a little dipstick built into the cap. Your mechanic, dealer, or parts store can tell you what fluid to use if you need to top off.

A modern automotive air conditioner is a rugged system which, when properly serviced, can be dependable for many years. The simplest service, which any driver can perform, is to turn on the air conditioner for at least five minutes once a week, winter and summer.

Operating the air conditioner circulates the freon refrigerant and the lubricants that are sealed inside and helps protect internal parts. It's also an easy way to test the switch, fuse, airflow linkage, drive belt, and compressor clutch. If you feel fully cold air, make a mental note to check the system again in a week. You have just performed preventive maintenance on an expensive system!

If you feel air that is only slightly cool, or no air at all, have your air conditioner serviced promptly by a shop that does this kind of work. The fault may be a blown fuse or a loose or broken belt. There may be a refrigerant leak which the technician can find and correct. Allowing the system to stand with insufficient refrigerant or lubricant can cause costly damage to the compressor.

As you recall when you bought your car, adding air conditioning was an expensive option. It's also an expensive repair. An annual A/C checkup can be a significant money saver.

Battery Basics: Keeping the Juice Flowing

Even though today's batteries are far better than their predecessors, there are few car owners who haven't experienced a "dead" battery. Many times, however, the culprit is not the battery, but the battery cables.

All the current that flows in your car is carried by your battery cables. One goes from your negative (-) battery terminal to a bolt on your engine block. The other starts at the positive (+) battery terminal and goes to the starter relay. About the only service these important cables ever need is to keep them clean and tight at both ends. Warm water, a brush, and dish detergent will clean the terminals. *Never use baking soda!* Use a plastic or wood-and-bristle brush to clean the battery and terminals when the battery is hooked up. Using a metal brush when the battery is hooked up can cause a dangerous shower of sparks if you inadvertently complete an electrical circuit. Look for corrosion around the battery connections. Corrosion can "break" an electrical circuit, leading you to assume your perfectly good battery is "dead." If cables are corroded, remove and clean them with fine sandpaper or steel wool. The inside of the connection and the battery posts should be shiny when you reconnect the cables.

If you have a battery with caps on the top, lift them off to see if the fluid comes up to the bottom of the filler neck. If it doesn't, add water (preferably distilled). If the temperature is freezing, add water only if you are planning to drive the car immediately. The newly added water can freeze and damage your battery. Not all batteries have filler caps. Some so-called "maintenance-free" batteries do not have refill caps and you never have to add water. However, these batteries have almost disappeared from the market.

"No matter what you've heard or read, never use baking soda for cleaning battery terminals! A battery contains strong sulfuric acid. Baking soda is an alkali. If the soda leaks into the battery through a crack, it can cause a colossal explosion. One of my customers underwent extensive plastic surgery after this kind of accident. Try warm water liquid dish detergent and a nonmetallic brush. It's safe and works like a charm."
T.K.

If you need to tighten the battery cable connections, you're perfectly safe at either end of the negative (-) cable. But when tightening either end of the positive (+) cable, your wrench *must not contact* any metal part of the car, or there will be an instantaneous and dangerous shower of sparks!

The Jump Start

There are few motorists who have never had to jump start a car because of a "dead" battery. Surprisingly, that innocent-looking battery can be the cause of serious injuries.

Batteries produce hydrogen gas when they discharge or undergo heavy use, such as cranking the engine for a long period of time. A lit cigarette or a spark can cause this gas to explode. Whenever you are working with the battery, always remove the negative (-) cable first. When you are done, reconnect it last. This will greatly reduce the chance of causing a spark that could ignite any hydrogen gas present.

For a safe jump start:

● Connect each end of the red cable to the positive (+) terminal on each of the batteries.

● Connect the end of the black cable to the negative (-) terminal of the good battery.

● Connect the other end of the black cable to the engine block (or exposed metal away from the battery) of the car being started. The reason for making that final connection to the engine block is to keep it as far as possible from the battery and dangerous hydrogen gas.

● To avoid damage to the electrical parts of the car being started, make sure the engine is running at idle speed before disconnecting the cables.

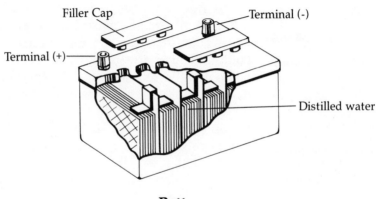

Filler Cap — Terminal (-)

Terminal (+)—

— Distilled water

Battery

Keep on Top of Your Tires

It sounds hard to believe, but the tire is one of the most complex items on the car. That round, black circle, that most of us take for granted, must simultaneously perform more functions than any other part of the car. These include maintaining contact with the road to bear the load, steering the car, transmitting power to the road, cushioning the ride and stopping the car. Furthermore, it is expected it to perform these tasks in all kinds of weather and on all kinds of roads.

There are two ways to check your tires for wear. Insert the top of a penny into a tread groove. If all of Lincoln's head is visible it's time to replace the tire. While this old rule of thumb is still valid, today's tires have a built-in wear indicator. A series of smooth horizontal wear bars will appear across the surface of your tire when the tread depth reaches the danger zone.

Improperly inflated tires are a major cause of premature tire failure. Check for proper inflation at least once a month. The most fuel-efficient inflation level is the maximum pressure listed on the side of the tire. Because many gas station pumps do not have gauges, and those that do are generally wrong, you should invest in your own tire gauge.

Tip: Register your new tires. The law once required all tire sellers to submit your name to the manufacturer, so the company could contact you if the tires were recalled. This is no longer required for independent tire dealers. Ask for the tire registration form when you buy tires and remember to fill it out and send it in. This is the only way a company can get in touch with you if your tires are recalled.

"Keeping your tires inflated to the maximum tire pressure is the single most important thing you can do to increase their life. Because most gas station air pumps are inaccurate, keep a tire pressure gauge in your glove box." J.G.

Extending the Life of Your Car

Two important adjustments that will double the life of your car cannot be made by your mechanic. Changing your driving habits and increasing your preventive maintenance efforts are adjustments that *you* can make.

Accelerating gently, anticipating and coasting to most stops, avoiding abrupt maneuvers, and driving the speed limit will eliminate most of the needless strain on your car's drive train, suspension, and brakes.

Following the manufacturer's recommended service schedule, especially for lubrication and oil changes, servicing wheel bearings, and inspecting the transmission and differential are all key to doubling your car's life. A word of caution: The owner's manual was written before your car went on the market, and reflects expected service requirements. However, your mechanic's experience, influenced by factory technical bulletins, may dictate modifications.

One of the reasons cars don't last is that they are engineered to be operated at more or less continuous speeds approaching the speed limit. But most of us rarely drive this way.

Most cars are driven in city or bumper-to-bumper freeway traffic. Often the speed is well below design optimums, usually in stop-and-go conditions for short periods of time. Typical driving actually causes the highest maintenance costs per mile and the most wear. There are a number of reasons, but two big ones are temperature and lubrication.

After an engine has run at full speed for fifteen minutes, it is fully warmed up. Any water that has condensed from vapor in the air is driven out of the engine oil. The lubricating oil thins to its design viscosity and is forced under pressure to every moving part of the engine that needs lubrication. Carbon and debris are flushed away from bearing surfaces

"I've seen 20 year-old cars with the original finish which run like a charm and 5 year-old cars that were totally beaten. The difference is always in how the owner cared for and drove the car." T.K.

"Even a small investment in preventive maintenance will pay off in lower repair costs." J.G.

91

to be captured eventually by the oil filter. Similar effects occur in the transmission, differential, universal or CV joints, axle and wheel bearings, speedometer cable, and countless other parts of the car.

If you typically drive on a stop-and-go basis, treat your car to a freeway trip at the speed limit for at least fifteen minutes every week.

PM—Two Initials for Long Life

All automobile manufacturers' owner manuals include suggested schedules of service which, if followed, will maintain a car's performance, appearance, and safety. When a car is new almost all owners are faithful about following the recommended schedule. As the car ages, preventive maintenance (PM) is usually neglected. Ironically, the older car may need service more often than the newer one.

A good maintenance schedule should include a number of checks. Your car's safety equipment should be looked at once or twice a year. This includes checking all of your lights, testing your brakes, tires, and checking the front end alignment. Window glass, windshield wipers and washers, horn, and turn signals should also be inspected. You can do much or all of the work yourself or your regular mechanic will do the job for a few dollars. Once in a while you'll hear of an advertised special offering a free safety inspection. The shop will do the testing free, gambling that you'll have them fix anything they find that's wrong, and that's a fair gamble.

All your fluid levels should be checked twice a year, or at the same time you change engine oil and filter. Wheel bearings are checked when your chassis is lubed. The most important thing is to adhere to a schedule.

Don't forget your car's appearance. Not only will keeping the inside and outside clean prevent rust and general deterioration, but add value when it comes time to sell.

Special Care for the "Middle-Aged" Car

The average automobile on the road is seven years old, so it's reasonable to think of a 7 year-old car as middle aged, with about half its hard life behind it. If you decide to keep your 7 year-old car, or buy someone else's, you should be aware of some special maintenance requirements.

• Tires: If you plan to continue driving an older car, check the tires. If they show wear, consider installing a new set.

• Brakes: Get a certified professional to check the entire braking system, not only the linings or pads, but the master cylinder, wheel cylinders, calipers (if your car has disc brakes), brake lines and flexible brake hoses. This may be a good time for a thorough pressure bleeding and flushing.

• Hoses: Check all the vacuum, fuel, upper and lower radiator, and heater hoses. You'll probably be surprised at how little this kind of maintenance will cost, especially if you do all or part of the work yourself. You'll add a great deal of reliability and safety.

• Drive train: Check the engine, transmission, drive shafts and universal or constant-velocity joints, and differential if the car has one. Spreading this work over a period of time will make it easier on your budget.

The appearance of the car can be improved by what is known as "detailing." Detailing originated as an intensive cleaning of automobiles by used car dealers. It proved to be a profitable investment, because the better-looking cars sold for higher prices. The name for the process evolved because attention was given to every detail of appearance.

Today's detailing industry is a sub-specialty that markets its services directly to the public as well as to dealers. You can easily locate a detailer in your telephone yellow pages, or your regular mechanic probably knows several.

The first step a detailer takes is to clean the car thorougly inside, outside, and under the hood. Special compounds and power tools are used to buff the paint and remove oxidized flakes. Then the paint is sealed with wax to protect it.

The interior, including upholstery and dash, are treated with special dressings to restore lost oils and maintain flexibility. Carpets and tires are cleaned and "dressed" thoroughly. The underhood area gets attention with solvents, cleaners, and spray cans of special paint.

Though safety items have the first priority, a detailed cleaning can make the older car more pleasant to drive.

Your Tool Kit **I**f you drive a car, sooner or later an emergency will arise. You can't anticipate every possible mishap, but *being prepared* is a good philosophy to follow.

The two most frequent causes of breakdowns are running out of gas and flat tires. You're rarely far from a service station, but you're often a long way from an open store that sells gas cans, especially at reasonable prices. So, carry an *empty* one-gallon gas can. Never carry a full gas can! That's worse than a trunk full of hand grenades.

For the flat tire, you'll need a good spare, a jack, and a lug wrench, all of which you can find in the dark. It may be reassuring too if you've practiced changing a tire in the safety of your own driveway.

A first aid kit also belongs in every car. It need not be elaborate, but it should be sealed. Next, carry a pack of at least three safety flares. If you've never lighted one of these, buy an extra and ignite it for practice, preferably over a clear concrete area. You won't want to be fumbling to learn how to use a safety flare during a real emergency. Other items to consider include a gallon of water, a quart of motor oil, and a small can of transmission fluid if your car uses it.

As far as tools go, here are some basic items: A strong pocket knife, a medium screwdriver, a good quality pair of pliers or Vise Grips, a few wrenches, and a flashlight. Don't forget to test your flashlight regularly. Wrapping everything in an old towel will keep it from rattling around and give you something to clean up with afterward.

If you own tire chains, keep them in your trunk throughout the winter. Stow a four-by-four foot plastic tarp near the chains, and perhaps an old blanket to kneel on, in case you're forced to install or remove your own. Carry an old towel as well, because installing tire chains can be a wet and dirty job. If you've never done it, you may want to practice on a dry day in the comfort of your driveway. We suggest keeping your chains in an old gym bag or duffel bag. That way they won't be a constant nuisance in your trunk.

One of the most versatile and important items in your tool kit is duct tape—the grey fabric stuff with the stick-to-anything adhesive. In an emergency it can patch up or hold a variety of things. More than one car has limped for many miles into a service shop with a ruptured water hose, held together temporarily with duct tape. A few strips can hold your trunk lid closed if it's overloaded or the latch is broken. You can even make the letters for a "Help" sign that's visible even at night because of the duct tape's reflecting qualities.

A small investment in some basic tools could mean the difference between waiting by a deserted road for assistance that may be hours in coming and a quick adjustment or repair that could get you back on the road. Even if you cannot make the repair yourself, a passenger or passerby may be able to assist you if you have some simple tools.

The Undriven Vehicle

Here are some tips to keep that rarely driven vehicle in top shape. The most important thing you should do is start the vehicle at least once a month and allow the engine to run long enough to fully warm up for at least fifteen minutes at idle. This will accomplish a number of objectives.

First, it will maintain the charge in your battery, important to preserving its life. Running the engine also flushes fresh gasoline through fuel lines and carburetor bowl. Stale gasoline in those places can oxidize and turn into a jelly, especially in the presence of condensation or contamination. Warming the engine thoroughly will remove any water or fuel that has condensed in the oil pan.

It's also a good idea to keep the gas tank full. This leaves less space for air in the tank and reduces the risk of water vapor condensing into the gasoline.

Move the vehicle at least two or three feet a month, to put the vehicle weight on a fresh portion of the tire tread. Be sure tires are kept at their proper inflation at all times. An ideal plan would be to drive to a service station maybe five miles from home, about once a month. There you can top off the gas tank and check tire inflation. By the time you get back home, the engine will be fully warm. Then check the water level in your battery, top it off with distilled water, and you're set for another month. Following these tips will help insure that your vehicle will be ready to start whenever you need it.

Wash and Wax

There is a right way and a wrong way to wash your car in order to avoid scratching your vehicle's expensive paint job. First of all, never dust off the car when the finish is dry. That's a sure way to make hundreds, even thousands of tiny scratches that will destroy the integrity of the paint's surface. The suds you use act as a lubricant as well as a detergent. Don't risk using household cleaners on your car. There are many excellent and inexpensive automobile detergents on the market. Using big, floppy, woolly mittens to swab the car off will make the process very efficient. Park in a shady spot and use plenty of warm, sudsy water from a bucket. Start with the top and work your way down saving the wheels for last. Never allow suds to dry on the paint. Hose off each section as you wash it.

When the job's completed, dry the entire car with the softest rags. The pros use a genuine chamois skin softened in water.

Windows will need special attention. You may want to use paper towels and a spray window-washing solution. Your parts store sells excellent spot removers, polishes, and conditioners for upholstery, chrome, and vinyl; follow package directions carefully.

If you notice nicks or deep scratches in the paint, fill them in. Your dealer or parts store sells perfectly matched paint in a small bottle with a brush inside, like nail polish. Finally, every car needs wax, even the ones with "no-wax" paint. One does not want to wax a car too seldom, nor too frequently. There are different waxes and different methods of application. Each type varies in the time, effort, and expense they demand. The "wipe on, wipe off" type, while comparatively easy to apply, doesn't offer the degree of protection or the durability of the more difficult "rub on, buff off" type.

Wax that is sprayed on at a car wash is least durable of all.

The shiny appearance of a wax job is actually only a fringe benefit. The real reason you wax is to protect the surface of the paint from harmful elements in the environment and abrasion from dust and dirt that hits your car when you drive.

To determine when to wax, observe what happens to your car's finish when it rains or when you sprinkle water on it. If water "beads up" or forms droplets that seem to roll off, you have enough wax protection. When water droplets no longer bead, you need more wax, no matter how long since your last wax job.

WHAT'S WRONG WHEN...

Generally your automobile will warn you before a major mechanical problem occurs. Paying attention to those signals can save you money. For example, a slight vibration in your steering wheel may be caused by something as simple as balancing weight falling off one of the front wheels. If you have it corrected promptly it will cost under ten dollars—ignore it and you might wear out your tire and need a front end alignment which could cost over $100.

An early warning signal could indicate more than one problem. A car which has become more and more difficult to start may have a sticking choke, a loose starter motor, a worn timing chain, or need an overdue tuneup. Taking the car to the repair shop will save you the cost of an untimely breakdown and a towing bill.

Many times subtle warning signals that would scream *danger* to a mechanic are ignored by a non-mechanic because they masquerade as minor annoyances. Diagnosing repair problems is one of the most valuable services a good mechanic can provide. Throughout the book we have stressed the importance of letting the mechanic do the diagnostic work and you just describing the symptoms. In this chapter we are offering some of the reasons for the car problems you may encounter. Reading through them now, or referring to them later, will help you better understand your car. Knowing *what's wrong when* . . . can help you keep repair costs to a minimum.

"A regular customer of mine was on his way to work with his new car when the red temperature warning light blinked from his dash. Since the light went out almost immediately, he assumed the problem wasn't serious. When it flashed on again for ten or fifteen seconds, he decided to drive to my shop. Unfortunately, it was the wrong decision. On the trip, the warning light came on and stayed on.

After passing at least twenty places that could have helped him, he arrived at my shop. I carefully removed his radiator cap and was surprised that there was no pressure. His lower radiator hose had fallen completely off and almost every drop of coolant was gone. I popped the hose back on and asked him to start the engine before I slowly added water. It was too late. The crankshaft bearings had seized and the starter motor couldn't turn the engine over.

We had to pull the engine out of the almost new car and completely rebuild it. Because he had ignored the "idiot" light to go one more mile, he voided his warranty. It cost him $900 to get back on the road." T.K.

Your Car Won't Start

Obviously, there are lots of reasons your car may not start. In this section, we discuss some of the more common problems.

If your car starts easily when the engine is cold, but cranks slowly and barely starts when it's hot, the problem may be in the starter. Your mechanic can confirm or rule it out by measuring the current draw of the starter. This symptom can be produced by a loose battery cable. There are four terminations, one at the end of each cable, and the slightest looseness at any point could be causing the problem.

Another reason for hard starting is an overheated engine. A hot engine is tighter and puts more load on a starter motor than a cool one. Modern pressurized cooling systems, permanent-type coolants, and coolant recovery tanks allow an engine to overheat considerably without any obvious boiling or loss of coolant. However, if you're low on coolant, the result could be hard starting. Remove the pressure cap on a thoroughly cool engine and check the actual level of the coolant in the radiator to see if this is the problem.

Whatever the cause of slow starting when the engine is warm, don't ignore it. If the engine is overheating, internal parts are being harmed. If you don't resolve the problem, it will appear again and will probably get worse, no matter how hard you try to ignore it.

If your problem is a cold engine that starts quickly, but stalls repeatedly, especially when put in gear, then runs fine when it warms up, the part that comes under suspicion is the choke vacuum pulloff. A cold choke thermostat forces the choke plate to fully close, cutting off all air to the engine until the engine starts to warm up. But in order to warm up, the engine has to run. In order to run, it needs a small amount of air, and in order to get air

"Never pour gasoline into a carburetor when trying to start an engine. Liquid gasoline, when splashed onto an engine, can produce a spectacular explosion. Instead, buy a can of starting fluid. It will start your car more readily and more safely than gasoline, even in cold weather, and is very easy to use." T.K.

while it's cold, something has to pull the choke plate open a tiny bit. The device that does this is the choke pulloff unit, which senses engine vacuum and opens the choke a few millimeters once the engine starts, no matter how cold it is.

When the vacuum pulloff units are separate units, bolted to the side of the carburetor and connected to the choke plate through an easy-to-trace linkage, they're easy to identify, diagnose, and replace. The problem is on cars with *integral* chokes. They look like little black plastic jar lids, built right into the carburetor. Usually the integral choke has a different type of pulloff device. The device is so small that you may miss it unless you know exactly where to look. Adjusting these devices requires a good shop manual, plus a generous supply of patience.

If your engine won't start and you're late for an appointment, relax. Here are a few tricks that may get you going. The most common reason a car won't start is that it's out of gas. If you drive off the top half of your tank, this won't happen. But fuel gauges can lie, and thieves can empty your gas tank. To find out, you may want to remove your air cleaner, look down the throat of your carburetor, and you should see a small, steady stream of fuel when you work the accelerator linkage.

After an empty tank, the most frequent starting failure culprit is corrosion of the pencil-diameter wire that runs from the center of the coil to the center of the distributor cap. Copper sulphate crystals can build up on the bronze terminals at either end. If you find a greenish-blue deposit on either end of the wire, scrape it off as best you can. A pocket knife, or even a paper clip will do the job. You don't need a perfect connection, just enough to get you started.

Probably the most common reason for a car not starting is cold weather. The fact is, a cold gasoline engine does not want to run. Cold gasoline does not vaporize readily, liquid gasoline will scarcely burn, and when it hits the cold metal of the cylinder wall, its natural tendency is to sit there and refuse to ignite.

To compound the problem, your battery is not as "powerful" in winter as in summer. In good condition and fully charged, a battery will have its optimum power at seventy-two degrees Fahrenheit. Reduce the temperature to a few degrees below freezing and that same battery loses 20 percent of its power.

Another factor with cold weather is that engine oil becomes thicker, does less to decrease friction, and doubles the power needed to turn the engine over.

So what you have on a moderately cold winter day is a battery that has lost 20 percent of its power, trying to turn over an engine that requires twice as much cranking power for a longer period of time before it will fire.

On a really cold day, say a few degrees below zero, the effect is more severe. The battery loses over half its power, the engine is three times as hard to turn over, and the gasoline even harder to vaporize. And that's why cars are harder to start in winter. It also explains why older batteries usually give up on winter rather than summer mornings.

Your Car Stalls or Backfires

Some cars are equipped with an emission control device known as a deceleration valve or "decel" valve, for short.

The decel valve is tucked neatly out of sight under the air filter near the carburetor and one end is connected to the intake manifold. The function of the decel valve is to inject fuel and air into the engine when the driver lets up on the gas to slow down. The result is cleaner exhaust emissions.

Problems result when an internal vacuum-sensing diaphragm punctures or cracks. If the diaphragm develops a hole, two bad things happen: a vacuum leak and failure of the decel valve. A vacuum leak into the manifold results in a drop off in mileage and power, overheating, and rough running, especially noticeable at low speeds.

To make matters worse, a hole in the diaphragm prevents the valve from doing its job of injecting fuel-air mixture under deceleration. The result can be stalling, backfiring, and noticeably rough running while slowing down.

An experienced technician can find a bad decel valve diaphragm in a few seconds and replace it in fifteen minutes or less. If a well-meaning, but uninformed, mechanic tries to resolve the problem by increasing the idle speed, the higher speed will mask the symptoms, but will not eliminate them. Furthermore, higher engine idle, especially with an automatic transmission, can be dangerous in traffic and cause premature brake wear.

S-T-O-P: A-OK!

In its early days, engine temperature, oil pressure, and battery charging rate were all monitored by dashboard gauges, or they were not monitored at all. Later these gauges were replaced by warning lights, which were often called "idiot" lights, an unfair misnomer. If such a light comes on in your car, it's necessary to interpret and act with common sense, because different lights require different actions.

Here is a phrase to help you remember what to do when a dashboard warning light goes on: S-T-O-P, A-OK. This means to "Stop for Temperature or Oil Pressure, Amps OK.

If your Amps or Alternator light is the one that comes on, there is a failure in your charging system. That merely means your battery is not being recharged. Turn off all electrical equipment, except headlights if you need them, and you can safely drive to get help. Your car will run for up to an hour or two, but it's wise not to turn off the engine. Starting is a heavy drain on the battery. So it's A-OK to continue driving for awhile if your alternator light comes on.

On the other hand, if your oil pressure light comes on, immediately take your foot off the gas, coast to the nearest safe parking place, and turn off the ignition. You're probably just low on engine oil. If you have some oil, put it in the engine, start up, and watch the warning light. If it does not go out within thirty seconds, stop the engine and call for help. Otherwise, drive slowly to a service station and top off your oil.

If your temperature light goes on, pull over safely, park, and turn off the engine. Wait for a full fifteen minutes, cautiously remove your radiator cap, and pour in some water. If you cannot get any water, wait the full fifteen minutes with the engine off and then drive the car toward help at moderate speed, so long as the light stays off. If it comes back on, stop again for another fifteen minutes of cooling. With luck, you should get a mile or more of driving for each fifteen minutes of cooling.

An engine with no oil pressure or a bad cooling system can destroy itself in a matter of minutes. That's the *S-T-O-P* part.

If your check engine light comes on, either your computer or one of the systems in your engine has sent what is known as a trouble code. Check your owner's manual for possible cause and be sure to have the problem identified and corrected.

S-T-O-P, A-OK!

You Have Carburetor Problems

It can be a monstrous waste of money to rebuild your carburetor, unless you're absolutely certain there's something wrong with it. Any time you suspect your carburetor, it's wise to pay for testing by a qualified, certified technician, in order to eliminate all the other possible causes.

It's a well-known fact among tuneup technicians that over 60 percent of customer complaints about carburetors can be resolved *without touching the carburetor.* Rebuilding your carburetor is expensive. So is buying a new one. Removing, replacing, and adjusting the carburetor add to the cost.

As fuel injection becomes universal, eliminating the use of carburetors, carburetor complaints will diminish and disappear. But it will be quite awhile before carburetors are gone forever. Just about every symptom that can be produced by a faulty carburetor can be duplicated by failure of some other part. An engine backfiring through the carburetor may be caused by a defective accelerator pump, improper timing, or a worn valve. Loss of power on acceleration could result from an accelerator pump malfunction or a punctured diaphragm in the distributor advance unit. If this problem is coming from a vacuum leak at the intake manifold, you'll notice a sound like a "backfire." Loss of power and poor mileage may mean a faulty carburetor or a hole in your PCV hose.

A sooty black deposit or black smoke from your exhaust pipe can be caused by a faulty or improperly adjusted float in your carburetor, or it may result from oil leaking past your valve guides. Defective electronics can produce each of these symptoms, sometimes simultaneously. Assuming that your carburetor needs to be replaced, could have been a costly mistake.

The Steering Wheel Vibrates

Here's the danger signal: You're driving at freeway speeds and you notice an unmistakable vibration in your steering wheel. It's never been there before, but now it won't go away. It's possible that it may be just a bumpy road or a lost wheel balance weight. It's also possible that you have a major problem with your front suspension system.

Since you can't tell what's wrong from inside the car, here's what you should do: Any time you detect an unusual vibration in your steering wheel, *slow down at once.* Move as far to the right side of the road as you safely can and slow to twenty miles per hour. At that speed, if a wheel falls off, you won't be hurt.

If you hear raw metal-on-metal sounds or if a wheel collapses, you'll have no choice but to stop and have the car towed. Otherwise keep your speed at or below twenty miles per hour and head for a repair shop.

Take the car to a shop that does tire work and wheel balancing, as well as front end work. Don't drive the car over twenty miles per hour until you get professional attention.

If a front wheel bearing on your car becomes worn or drifts out of adjustment, it can produce a number of symptoms. Loose or improperly tightened wheel bearings can cause play in your steering. A cracked or flattened wheel bearing can make your car pull to one side when you apply brakes. Bearing wear can produce vibration, which sometimes changes when brakes are applied. Some types of wear can cause the car to wander.

Wheel bearings are long-lived and dependable. It is not unheard of for a car to run its entire life and go to the wrecking yard with the original factory wheel bearings still in place, provided they've been periodically serviced. In normal use, we recommend that wheel

"Have you noticed on freeway pavement those long, curving black skid marks that sweep to the side of the road? That's what can happen when a front suspension fails." T.K.

"Most front end problems are minor and easily repaired. But, you'll never know how serious it is until a professional checks it out." J.G.

bearings be serviced every 20,000 miles, which is somewhat more often than most car manufacturers recommend. Using special tools, your regular mechanic will do the job for just a few dollars. Bearings should also be serviced every time your brakes are serviced. Wheel bearings are tough and reliable, but for safety and economy, they must be taken care of.

Clearly, each of the above-mentioned symptoms could be caused by a different problem. If your car ever develops any of these symptoms, have it checked out at once by a technician certified in front end repair. More than likely, the problem can be solved with an adjustment or minor repair. However, if it's not, the professional inspection will have helped avoid a dangerous situation.

Your Engine Overheats

The most common causes of engine over-heating are loss of coolant, a faulty thermostat, or a broken belt. If your engine is overheating, check your coolant recovery tank first. As the engine runs, the coolant in the system heats up and expands, and its excess flows through a tube to a recovery tank. Later, when the engine cools off, the coolant contracts and the reserve coolant is drawn back into the radiator. If the tube works loose or splits, coolant will leak each time it passes through. Air can also enter the cooling system which can cause a number of problems.

To find your car's coolant recovery tank, start at the radiator cap and trace the small hose. You'll come to a container with markings that say *Full Hot* and *Full Cold*. The coolant level should be between those marks.

Overheating is also caused by sediment in the cooling system. If that happens, the system may need to be reverse-flushed and refilled. Sediment can also damage the water pump, thermostat, and hoses, so they should all be checked.

You may also have a problem with your radiator pressure cap. If your pressure cap is not working, your coolant will boil away. Unpressurized plain water will boil away at 212 degrees. A pressurized coolant mixture won't boil until it reaches 260 degrees or so.

If your cooling system checks out, then your tuneup settings should be checked to be sure that the fuel-air ratio is correct, the timing is right, and the emission control system is functioning properly. Finally, check your oil to be sure it's clean and filled to the proper level with the right oil. Also check to see if the oil filter is clogged. In addition to lubricating, oil also cools the engine.

Your Fan Stops—or Won't Stop

There are basically two types of fans: those connected by a belt directly to the engine and electric fans with their own motor. Fans connected directly to the engine do not rotate unless the engine is running. An electric fan is run by a thermostat. It turns on when the water in the radiator reaches a certain temperature. That's why it may not always be running when your engine is. That's also why it may turn on, or keep running, after you've turned off the engine. It may surprise you to hear your fan turn on as you walk away from your car. Don't worry—that means it's doing its job. Be careful when checking out your fan because it could start unexpectedly—even when the ignition switch is off.

There are two ways the electric fan can go awry: Either it won't run, which can result in overheating; or it won't stop, which can result in a dead battery. Failure to run may be caused by a bad motor, a loose wire, a blown fuse, or a defective sensor. If it doesn't stop, it could be because of a shorted sensor or relay. Your mechanic will need a voltmeter or test light and the wiring diagram for the car to check out a problem.

The electric fan has a number of advantages. It can run at full speed when it is needed most, in slow, stop-and-go traffic. When it is not needed, as at freeway speeds, it can turn off and remove its load from the alternator which improves mileage. The belt-driven fan can't do either of those things.

Your Brakes Are Making Noise

If you hear a metallic sound when you apply brakes, ignoring it could cost you needless expense and be a safety risk. On some makes of cars with disc brakes, there's a sensor to warn you when your pads are so thin they must be replaced. The sensor is a finger of soft steel. When pad wear allows it to contact your brake rotor, it produces an irritating, high-pitched squeal. Ask your regular mechanic if your car has disc-brake sensors. If you ever hear the sound, you should get your brake pads replaced within the next fifty to 100 miles.

If your car has drum brakes or standard disc brakes, any metal-on-metal sound will be lower pitched, more jarring, and much more serious. Reduce your speed to no more than twenty miles per hour and proceed directly to a brake shop, shifting down to use engine compression for deceleration as much as possible. That harsh sound indicates that your pads or shoes are worn through, and the metal base is grinding away at your expensive rotor or drum.

Your brake technician can remove minor damage from rotor or drum by putting either on a lathe and removing a layer of metal, but there's a rigid limit to the amount one can legally "turn" off. Driving with metal grinding on metal can cause that much wear in a few miles, which means the drum or rotor must be replaced. This will dramatically increase the price of the repair.

To avoid this misfortune, have your brakes inspected periodically, and have them serviced when they're past 80 percent of their useful life. That way, you'll never hear that costly and unwelcome metal-on-metal screech.

Brakes in all cars manufactured in the last twenty-five years are redundant. That means the hydraulic system is split, either fore-

"If your vehicle behaves in an unfamiliar manner, especially if it involves gasoline, brakes, or front suspension, phone a towing company and ask the price to have your car towed to the nearest repair shop. Then imagine yourself in an accident, miles from home, and ask if you would pay the price of the tow to avoid the accident. Often, that's your real choice." T.K.

114

and-aft or diagonally, so that if one half of the system fails, the other half will stop the car. There's also a mechanical backup, the parking brake.

Most cars have a brake warning light. When the parking brake is set and the ignition switch is on, the brake warning light comes on, and in some cars it flashes.

If the brake warning light comes on with the parking brake *off*, the ignition on, and the brake pedal depressed, it's alerting you that pressure is low in some part of the brake system. If this happens, you should drive slowly to a nearby shop that works on brakes. Your safety factor is gone because if the other half of the system should fail, you'd have no foot brakes.

If you ever depress the brake pedal and your car won't stop, pump it several times quickly. If you still don't stop, apply the parking brake, hard. This can produce a jarring stop, so be aware of cars behind you. Once you're safely out of traffic, don't drive the car another foot! Have it towed to a brake shop.

If your car does not have a brake warning light, be alert for increased pedal travel. If the pedal goes down farther than usual, that's a sign that fluid is low in the entire system, or that one half of the dual system has failed. In either case, you'll want your brakes checked at once by a certified professional.

If Your Brakes Fail

What should you do to stop safely if you discover you have no brakes? If such an emergency should arise, there's rarely time for thoughtful consideration. You must react immediately with the proper emergency procedure—and that means you must do your thinking in advance.

First, whether your car has automatic or standard transmission, shift at once into the lowest gear. Engine compression will slow the car faster than you think. You should practice this maneuver, but be sure you're on a safe road, with no traffic behind you as you will slow down *quickly!*

Next, remember that your hand or parking brake is a mechanical system completely independent of the hydraulic brakes. Apply the hand brake *hard.* If you depress the release lever at the same time you apply the hand brake, you can achieve some control. This is another maneuver it would be wise to practice in a safe place. If you experience actual hydraulic brake failure, using these emergency procedures can help you stop safely. Remember: Don't drive a car on which the brakes have failed. Have it towed to a brake shop.

Gasoline is Leaking

If you notice gasoline leaking, you may be filling your tank too full.

Filling your tank to the top of the fuel filler neck is a mistake many people make. The filler neck of a gas tank and the input tube of the car are connected by a flexible neoprene tube, clamped at both ends. In time, the neoprene can deteriorate, and the clamps can loosen, causing a small amount of fuel to leak when the tank is overfilled.

When you fill up, insert the nozzle of the gas pump as far down into the filler tube as it will go. When it kicks off the first time, stop filling. Although you may be able to get another gallon in, more than likely most of it will end up on the ground.

Another reason your gas may be leaking is because you don't have a gas cap. Most cars have the gas cap hidden behind a little door. If you don't pump your own gas, you may not realize it's missing. If your gas tank is part of a sealed system and your gas cap is missing, your fuel and vapor return features will not work properly. You also may contaminate your fuel tank with water, leaves, twigs, and dust. If water in your gas tank is drawn into the carburetor fuel bowl, the combination can ruin the carburetor body and form a jellylike deposit that can harden like concrete.

If your gas cap is ever lost or stolen, head for a dealer or an auto parts store and replace it at once. It's cheaper than curing the many problems that may result. As a precaution, add a pint of gas drier, just in case any water got in.

"I recall one late model car that was driven without a gas cap for only a few weeks in Douglas Fir country. So many evergreen needles gathered that they plugged the pickup in the tank and starved the engine. When we removed and cleaned out that tank, we took out nearly a gallon of needles." T.K.

Engine Power Loss, Headlight Failure or Fire

If your car suffers severe, unexplained power loss, try this test: Holding a rag about a foot behind your tail pipe, have someone start the car, put it in neutral and step on the gas. If you don't feel and hear exhaust gas, your exhaust system is plugged which causes a severe loss of engine power.

If the exhaust system is fully or partially plugged, the car may exhibit many different types of problems. With nowhere for the exhaust gases to escape properly, there's no room in the cylinders for the fresh, unburned fuel/air mixture. The engine starves. It may sputter along at idle and low speed, but it can't accelerate to full power.

There are a number of ways your exhaust system could become blocked. If your car is backed into a clay bank and parked, the heat can bake the clay into a firm brick inside the exhaust pipe. The exhaust system can be severely dented by hitting an unusually high curb or a large rock on the road. Using leaded gasoline can plug up your catalytic converter. Finally the inside of the muffler can deteriorate and become stopped up.

Your Headlights Go Out

On most cars, changing headlights from high beam to low beam is accomplished by pressing a dimmer switch located on the floor board or a lever on the steering column. In time, heavy use or exposure to changing elements may cause the switch to fail.

If the switch is broken, the first thing you will usually notice is that using it will cause the headlights to go out. A frantic kick or a vigorous wiggle will usually restore headlights. After that, the switch may even work correctly, but don't be lulled into trusting it.

"I've had owners tow their cars to my shop after they've spent hundreds of dollars on unneeded fuel pumps, carburetors, distributors, and tuneups only to discover that the exhaust system was blocked." T.K.

Once a dimmer switch begins to go bad, it will continue doing so, often intermittently, until it gets a driver in serious trouble. With a little help from an auto parts store, you can replace the dangerous dimmer switch yourself. The kind on the floor is considerably easier than the ones in the steering column. If you don't want to tackle the job, your regular mechanic can do it for a few dollars.

Your Car Is on Fire

If you ever have a fire under the hood of your car, stop and turn off the engine as quickly as possible. Turning off the engine turns off the fuel pump, preventing more gasoline from being added to the fire. Next, get yourself and everyone else out of the car, and get back a safe distance, at least a hundred feet away. Do *not* try to put out the fire! Call a fire department and wait for them to arrive. If you open the hood, you may provide a smoldering fire enough oxygen to produce a fireball. In addition, the hood release may be hot enough to produce third degree burns on your hand.

Your Steering Wheel Pulls to One Side

You can avoid major expenses by being attentive to the minor symptoms your car displays. One of the easiest symptoms to ignore is the need to apply a little pressure to your steering wheel in order to keep your car going straight on level pavement.

That nagging pull on your steering wheel can have dozens of causes, some of them dangerous. Most of the time the reason will be that one front tire has lower air pressure than the other. If the difference is enough for you to notice at the steering wheel, it's costing you money. One tire may be overinflated, the other underinflated, or both. In any case, if you drive very far, you will prematurely wear out at least one tire.

Drive to a shop or service station and check the air in all four tires. If the tires are hot, the natural result of being driven, do *not* "bleed" air out to reduce pressure. Next morning, you may want to recheck cold tires, driven only a few miles. Driving tires at the proper pressure, you'll extend their lives by many miles.

One problem with keeping your tire pressure at the right level is that most gasoline station air pumps are inaccurate. We recommend that you keep a tire gauge in your glove compartment. One of the best rated and least expensive gauges is available from the Tire Industry Safety Council. Send $2 to the Council, Box 1801, Dept. AM, Washington, D.C. 20013 and ask for their tire gauge and information booklet.

"I check my tires once every month, and before leaving on any trip over a hundred miles." T.K.

RIPOFF TIPOFFS

Despite popular mythology, most mechanics are reliable and honest. This is not to say there's not an occasional ripoff. They happen. Sometimes even the customer contributes to what is later perceived as a ripoff. For example, if the mechanic is told, "I'm going on a trip. Fix whatever needs fixing," does the technician change all four spark plugs and check the tires, or does he replace all the worn parts that are discovered? If the mechanic finds dangerous tie-rod ends and worn-out brakes, and presents a bill for $300 for "authorized" work, the customer's first thought may be, "Ripoff!"

Surely, the mechanic was at fault. He should have phoned the customer and had the work specifically authorized. But the customer also contributed by not getting a written estimate in advance.

Before you allow work to be done on your car, even before you begin to deal with a shop, look out for these four red flags:

- They want to work without explaining the testing.
- They will not furnish a written diagnosis.
- They claim they can't furnish an estimate before starting.
- They make an alarmist statement without showing you the specific problem, such as, "Well, I wouldn't drive that car around the block the way it is now."

If you hear any of these, then chances are you are being "setup." It's not any one element that does it, but when all four are present, that's a surefire *ripoff tipoff.*

Of course, many repairs do not require testing. It doesn't take much testing to spot a blown-out tire or a ruptured radiator hose.

121

Similarly, at small shops customers will often say "Fix it" after being shown the problem, then wander off before a written estimate is prepared. And any conscientious shop will try to frighten the daylights out of you if they discover dangerously worn suspension parts or a gasoline leak—but they will insist on showing you the defects.

This section provides tipoffs to some of the potential ripoffs you may encounter. We certainly don't recommend that you approach every dealing with a mechanic fearing the worst. However, forewarned is forearmed!

"I'm glad to report that I profited from following my own advice. A few years ago my wife and I were driving on a lightly traveled road in California, between Interstate 5 and the Monterey Peninsula. About seven miles past the tiny town of Gilroy, and fifteen miles before we reached Watsonville, the car's water pump failed. After finding a telephone, we started calling shops and service stations in Gilroy. The first was too busy to help. The second had no road service truck. The third would do the job, but the price they quoted was far too high. On the fourth call, we found the right place. When the truck arrived it was spotlessly clean, and the mechanic wore an immaculate white shop coat. His workmanship was unhurried, but brisk and efficient. When we paid the bill he even refused a tip. The cost: we got a new water pump at 10 percent off and paid fifteen dollars for the mechanic to drive seven miles and install it. Moral of the story: Even when you're broken down on the freeway, in the middle of nowhere, in an unfamiliar area, it pays to comparison shop and to ask for the price in advance—even if you must do it by telephone!" T.K.

Advertised Specials

Often, problems arise when the specifics of an advertised special are not spelled out. For example, a front-end alignment advertised for $14.95 plus parts could easily cost you $100 if you have a worn suspension. Be sure to ask for a parts estimate *before* any work is done—then decide if you really want the special.

There's a national chain that used to advertise automotive mufflers for $19.95, installed. Because the actual wholesale cost of the muffler was over twenty dollars, the fine print told the real story: *additional parts at regular prices.* You could buy the muffler for $19.95, but if the company installed it, it would automatically replace your exhaust pipe, hangers, and tail-pipe at the same time. The actual cost was well over $100.

Another special to watch out for is the $1.99 lube job. While your car is on the hoist, you can be sure that the attendant will ask if you want an oil and filter change, at the regular price. Also expect the mechanic to check your universal joints, suspension, brake lines, and wheel cylinders for leakage. If the shop is reputable and the mechanic discovers a dangerous condition, you'll thank him. However, if you know your car is okay and you are only in for the special, expect some high-pressure selling. If you question the shop's honesty, get a second opinion.

Advertised bargains shouldn't always be avoided. A good repair shop wants you to come back again, so it will happily offer a true bargain to attract you for the first time. However, it also wants to know in advance how much your total job will cost. It will honor your request for a written estimate and answer your questions fully. A good shop wants you to understand its advertising, including the *fine* print.

"Although not all low-cost come-ons are ripoffs, you won't know until it's too late—unless you read the fine print." J.G.

123

"Can't Tell the Cost Until We Tear Into It"

If a mechanic ever tells you that, get out of that shop at once! Automobile repair shops base their charges on three items: testing, parts, and labor. Every shop can tell you how much a test will cost, and sometimes a test might be *necessary* to give you an accurate cost estimate.

After the test, the cost of your job will be based on parts and labor. You are entitled to know in advance the price of the parts for your job and every good shop will tell you if you ask.

The remaining item is labor. The labor charge is based on an hourly rate times the expected length of time to do the job. The hourly wage is always available and the time is usually determined by referring to a flat-rate book. This book lists thousands of repairs and the estimated time for each. At your request, most shops are willing to show you the listing for your job in their flat-rate manual. So there is no reason why a shop shouldn't tell you the cost of repairs once the problem is diagnosed.

If you allow a mechanic to take your engine apart to determine a particular problem, you're going to have to pay him to put it back together, whether or not you have the repair made. So, don't allow any major work to be performed on your car without knowing, in advance, what it will cost.

Ask to See the Test

Consider this: An agitated young woman drives into a gas station and asks the attendant to check her car because it had been "running funny." The mechanic pokes under the hood and says, "Lady, you're lucky you made it this far. You need a complete valve job. Cost? About $300." With serious misgivings, she drives off and limps into another shop. The second mechanic raises the hood and in two minutes has her malfunction corrected. A spark-plug wire and distributor wire were loose, causing the engine to vibrate and run roughly. The mechanic replaced the plug wire and set the timing—and charged the woman $8.50. At best, the first mechanic made a careless diagnosis. At worst, he was a ripoff artist.

How do you protect yourself in this kind of situation? To provide an accurate price for your repairs, your mechanic may have to do some *testing,* for which you should expect to pay a reasonable and predictable fee.

The fact is, for almost anything that can go wrong with a motor vehicle, there is a test to prove it. Remember the adage: *Test, don't guess.* Never patronize a mechanic who relies on guesswork or "feel." If you have *any* doubts about the diagnosis, get a second opinion from another shop. It's especially important to consider getting a second opinion if you are not working with your usual mechanic. If major repairs are suggested, make sure the small components of the problematic part have been tested. Sometimes a "minifix" will do the job. For example, if you're told you need a new carburetor, be sure your mechanic has tested your *choke thermostat,* your *vacuum pulloff,* and your *preheater.* Maybe you need the $150 new carburetor treatment. But it may be that the ten-dollar cure will do!

"If you came in to my shop and really needed a valve job, we would hook up my test equipment and show you how we knew which valves were bad." T.K.

"That's what you should look for—a shop that uses test equipment and is willing to explain the tests until you understand them." J.G.

125

"Guaranteed to Improve Your Mileage"

The best way to improve your car's mileage is with low-cost or no-cost common-sense procedures. Be on guard against expensive ripoffs. Every do-it-yourself magazine is filled with dozens of ads for items that are supposed to produce from 10 to 30 percent better gas mileage. That's the *ripoff tipoff.*

Auto manufacturers are ferociously competitive. If any of these gadgets actually worked, they would quickly become standard equipment on today's cars.

Many times the product may actually improve your mileage—but so would far less expensive alternatives. For example, a recent ad for "high-performance" spark-plug wires guaranteed improved mileage. Defective spark-plug wires will definitely decrease your gas mileage. Therefore, installing the advertised, overpriced, fancy-colored, high-performance wires, at a cost of sixty dollars, would improve your gas mileage. However, you could get the same improvement, for six or seven dollars, by replacing the bad wires with standard new ones.

The easiest things you *can* do to improve your mileage are to keep your engine in tune and your tires fully inflated. Modest measures such as these don't sound dramatic, but they're realistic. If you achieve a 10-percent mileage improvement, the savings is as good as buying your gasoline at a 10 percent discount—and you haven't been ripped off in the process.

Don't Let the Guarantee Rip You Off

There's a growing trend in the auto repair business to offer meaningful guarantees. But they're not all alike. You can be sure that the owner of a repair shop, and probably his attorney, has given thought to the terms of the shop's guarantee. As a customer, it's to your advantage to ask plenty of questions about a guarantee to make sure you understand it.

The only way to know and prevent an unnecessary ripoff is to read your warranty and ask questions before you buy. Find out what's covered and what's not and exactly what you have to do to get repairs done.

Advertised warranties are often just for the parts. If they fail, you may get free replacements but have to pay the labor charges for removing and replacing the items.

Sometimes the shop will actually guarantee its service. For example, it will guarantee that your car will stay in tune for a certain period of time after a tuneup. You'll want to know how long, in months and miles, the guarantee lasts and if the guarantee includes parts. If you are expected to buy replacement parts, make sure you can buy them at the original price.

Finally, on longer warranties, find out what happens if you sell the car before the warranty expires. (Most of the time the coverage stops.)

Beware of Counterfeit Parts

A counterfeit auto part is one that is packaged in a box printed to look like that of an advertised brand. The counterfeit boxes will rarely carry the name and address of the manufacturer or distributor. Counterfeit parts are not to be confused with legitimate and reliable "aftermarket" parts that are simply made by an honest auto parts company instead of the original manufacturer.

There are a number of ways for you to be sure you're buying quality parts. Original equipment manufacturer (OEM) parts are generally marketed by new car dealers and will be the same quality as those used at the factory. Many aftermarket brands are at least as good as, and often better and cheaper than, OEM parts. Most advertised brands, the ones you've heard of, are reliably good. Many large chain stores have enough buying power to purchase parts that are made by famous manufacturers and marketed at lower prices as "private-label" brands of the chain. These parts can represent excellent savings. The box will say "made for" or "distributed by" the name and address of the chain. Remember, counterfeit parts will not carry the name and address of the seller.

Ripoff tipoff: Check the boxes that your old parts are returned in to see if they match the description for counterfeit boxes.

"Beware of and avoid look-alike, counterfeit auto parts. They're about as good as counterfeit money." T.K.

128

A Shocking Discovery

Here is one of the oldest cons in the book: With your car up on the hoist, the mechanic calls you over and says, "Look. There's oil on your shocks. They're so worn the oil is coming out of them. We'll have to put on new ones, or it will void the warranty on your tires. Besides, it's so dangerous that you could lose your steering in the next block or two."

If anyone ever pulls the "oil on your shocks" ploy on you, recognize it as a *ripoff tipoff,* and demand the real test. Or simply leave. Oil on your shocks does not prove that they're bad— or good. It simply proves that there's oil on your shocks. It doesn't even prove that the bad guy sprayed it there!

You can easily tell if your shock absorbers are worn. Put your full weight on one corner of the car, for example by standing on the bumper. Then jump off. The car should bounce once above its resting position, once slightly below, and then stop. If it does this, the shock at that corner of the car is okay. Repeat the test for each corner.

Emergency Repairs: A Long Distance Ripoff Tipoff

If your car breaks down and you're in unfamiliar territory, here are some simple precautions to help avoid needless costs and aggravation.

First, don't panic and make snap judgments because you're in a hurry. Accept the reality that you will be delayed and don't compound the problem by allowing yourself to be cheated. Phone your destination to let someone know you'll be delayed. That will take some pressure off and make you less susceptible to a ripoff. Then look for nearby help.

The corner service station you coasted into may be a den of thieves, or it may be the most honest shop for miles around. Here's how to tell. The honest mechanic is going to perform some tests to find out with certainty what's wrong. He may well charge you for the tests, but he'll tell you those charges beforehand. He'll also allow you to watch, and he'll explain anything you don't understand. Finally, he'll put his diagnosis in writing, give you a firm, written estimate, and he'll *guarantee* that the work he proposes to do will eliminate your symptoms.

The honest shop won't mind if you ask to telephone your regular mechanic to read him the diagnosis and estimate and to ask if he thinks they sound reasonable. If the shop you're dealing with won't do these things, that's a *ripoff tipoff!*

This is a good time to reemphasize the importance of having a regular mechanic— a repair shop where you are a known and valued customer. This may never be more important than when you have trouble with your car and you're a distance from your regular shop. When you call your regular mechanic, describe your symptoms as best you can, then put the strange technician on the line with

"I've told my good, steady customers to call me, collect if necessary, in an emergency. We've also suggested to tourists who were afraid of a ripoff in my shop that they phone their own mechanic back home and let me talk with him." T.K.

your regular mechanic. Good mechanics everywhere use just about the same test procedures, the same tools, the same repair methods, and even describe them with the same jargon. An honest mechanic can recognize another honest mechanic. More important, he can spot a *ripoff tipoff* or an overcharge almost every time. Again, if the strange mechanic refuses to talk to your mechanic, he has just revealed something very important about himself!

Ripoff tipoff: If you're across town, a taxi ride to work and the bill to tow your car to your regular mechanic may be a lot easier to absorb than a $300 to $400 ripoff.

"Don't Worry —They All Do That"

It's just not true. Cars don't all shimmy, or start hard, or have a vibration in the transmission, and any mechanic who tells you they do ignores the truth that no car manufacturer could stay in business marketing vehicles with such obvious defects.

Problems almost never "solve themselves" as cars are driven. What a mechanic is really telling you when he says "Drive it and see if it straightens out" or "They all do that" is, "This problem is beyond my ability or willingness to diagnose and repair." That's an acceptable answer if he hasn't charged you anything. But it's wrong if your money is in the mechanic's pocket. If you hear either of these phrases, don't be a victim—refuse to pay, or demand a refund. You're entitled to results for your money. An auto repair shop is not a wishing well!

Ripoff tipoff: When you hear, "Brakes sometimes do that when they're new," "Drive the car a while and see if it straightens out," or "Drive it and see if the trouble cures itself," beware.

Repair Protection by Credit Card

Paying auto repair bills by credit card can provide much needed recourse if you are having problems with an auto mechanic. The Federal Trade Commission provides the following example of a situation where paying by credit card could save the day.

Suppose you take your car to the mechanic because of a noise in the power steering. The shop does a rack-and-pinion overhaul. You pay $180 with your credit card and drive home. The next afternoon, the noise is back. Another mechanic looks at the car and finds that the real problem was fluid leaking from the power-steering pump. That will cost another $125 to repair.

What happens if the first mechanic refuses to make good on his mistake? If you had paid the bill with cash, you would be out $180 and might have to file suit to recover your money. If you paid by check, it would probably be too late to stop payment. Payment with a credit card not only gives you extra time, but is also an effective tool for negotiating with the mechanic.

According to federal law, you have the right to withhold payment for sloppy or incorrect repairs. Of course, you may withhold no more than the amount of the repair in dispute.

In order to use this right, *first try to work out the problem with the mechanic.* Also, unless the credit-card company owns the repair shop (this might be the case with gasoline credit cards used at gas stations), two other conditions must be met: The repair shop must be in your home state (or within 100 miles of your current address), and the cost of repairs must be over fifty dollars.

Until the problem is settled or resolved in court, the credit-card company cannot charge you interest or penalties on the amount in dispute.

If you decide to take such action, send a letter to the credit-card company, with a copy to the repair shop, explaining the details of the problem and what you want as settlement. Send the letter by certified mail with a return receipt requested.

Sometimes the credit-card company or repair shop will attempt to put a "bad mark" on your credit record. You may not be reported as delinquent if you have given the credit-card company notice of your dispute. However, a creditor can report that you are disputing your bill and this can go in your record. The Fair Credit Reporting Act gives you the right to learn what information is in your file and challenge any information you feel is incorrect. You also have the right to have your side of the story added to your file.

Using a credit card will certainly not solve all your auto repair problems, but it can be a handy ally. For more information about your credit rights, you can write to the Federal Trade Commission, Credit Practices Division, Washington, DC 20580.

MYTHS AND MYSTERIES

Combine the idolatry that many of us have for automobiles with the reality that many of us don't truly understand these machines, and it's not too surprising that an entire mythology of mysterious misconceptions has arisen around the car. Some of them would be humorous—if they weren't so expensive.

This section explores some of the myths and mysteries. We have included them so that you'll know that, when it comes to cars, *all is not as it seems.* These stories should help you to avoid scams and keep you from inadvertently damaging your car.

Mechanics like to cite the infamous "brother-in-law" as the source of many of these inaccurate notions. The reason: customers often have mechanics correct problems that were caused by following procedures that were supposedly suggested by the customer's brother-in-law. We suspect that this relative isn't always the culprit. Nevertheless, these stories get passed around, and it's the unsuspecting car owners who end up doing costly damage to their cars.

One of the most common misconceptions that most of us have is the definition of *average driving conditions.* When the owner's manual suggests that the oil and filter should be changed after a certain number of miles under *average* driving conditions, drivers assume that the way they drive is average. The fact is, most of us do not drive under average conditions.

For example, a car may seat five, but it's engineered for an average load of two people with an empty trunk. Average conditions assume you drive with no more than one passenger, no luggage in the trunk, at a consistent speed on a paved highway, in fair weather with light winds and moderate temperatures, and each time you go out, your trip is at least 100 miles. The stop-and-go, around-town driving that most of us actually do is considered a severe driving condition and reduces your service intervals!

"Here is a brother-in-law story: I had a trusting customer who had his station wagon towed in for carburetor work. On the advice of his brother-in-law, he had sawed off the inlet threads of the built-in filter. That destroyed his carburetor, but we fixed him up. A few months later he was back again with a worn timing chain and gears, worn valves, and cylinder heads in need of conditioning. This was an older car, and I was dubious about doing the work, but quoted him a price and he gave me the go-ahead.

Two weeks later, he came in, totally disgusted. The engine had almost no power and heavy blue smoke poured from the exhaust. Before he took the thirty-five dollars a wrecking yard had offered him for the car, he asked me to check it out.

I expected to find broken rings or a cracked piston, but a cylinder efficiency test showed all eight were evenly balanced. My lead mechanic and I spent every spare moment for two days trying to figure this one out. I ran numerous tests, but found no clues.

At last, I disconnected the fuel line and pumped a pint or so of fuel into a can. That solved the mystery. It wasn't gasoline, it was diesel oil! The trusting owner, I learned, had heard from his brother-in-law that diesel fuel was more economical than gasoline, so he made a diesel conversion—by pouring diesel fuel into his gas tank! I cleaned the tank and installed a new set of spark plugs and the car still runs." T.K.

Tuneup Tales and Legends

In the past, tuneups were recommended every 10,000 miles. This interval is no longer valid. The best way to know when your car needs to be tuned up is to keep track of your miles per gallon. If your mileage drops below your average by 10 percent and stays there for three consecutive fill-ups, your car probably needs a tuneup. If it's just a bad spark-plug wire or some other simple problem, your mechanic will spot it the instant he tests with the oscilloscope, which should be a preliminary part of your tuneup.

If your car has an electronic ignition, you may have been told that it doesn't need to be tuned up. The truth is, you still need a tuneup, but the parts and procedures are different from a "conventional" tuneup.

Another myth about tuneups is how much they should cost. Here's a scenario that not only offends the professional mechanic but cheats the unknowing car owner as well: A customer gets a major tuneup for eighty-five dollars and drives away pleased in a car that is running noticeably more smoothly and economically than before. Then a friend or relative says, "Eighty-five dollars! You were ripped off. I could have done that job for eight dollars." The seed of doubt is planted, and as his reward for doing a thorough job at a reasonable price, the mechanic unfairly loses a customer.

The eight dollars might have covered the cost of four new spark plugs from a discount parts store, but a major tuneup includes much more than that. The mechanic installs new plugs, replaces the points and condenser (if the car has them), the distributor cap and rotor, the PCV valve, the fuel filter, and the air filter. Using the oscilloscope and exhaust analyzer, he adjusts the "dwell angle," if applicable, the carburetor or fuel-injection system, and the timing. If there's a computer, it is checked out and any trouble codes are interpreted, corrected, and reset. The EGR valve is checked and mileage warning device is reset. All fluid levels are topped up, the charging system is evaluated, and the battery is cleaned. Finally, the belts and wires are checked, and the car is test driven. The parts alone can typically cost fifty dollars.

If you ever suspect a ripoff, go back to the shop and allow the mechanic a chance to explain. If you don't like the answers, find another mechanic. But don't ever believe that an eighty-five dollar tuneup can be done for eight dollars!

Carburetor Misconceptions

Many car owners with V-8 engines have "four-barrel" carburetors. If that includes you, then you may have heard that replacing your four-barrel carburetor with a two-barrel model will save fuel. This is simply not true. In fact, a four-barrel carburetor, by design, is more fuel efficient than the two-barrel.

If, on the other hand, you have a two-barrel carburetor, you may be told that "only one of your throttles is opening and you'll have to have your carburetor replaced." Beware: The two-stage, two-barrel carburetor works exactly like *one side* of a four-barrel carburetor. This was one of the rare engineering breakthroughs that produced both increased power potential and improved economy, factors that usually contradict each other. Except under heavy loads or at high speed, a two-barrel, two-stage carburetor is supposed to have only one throttle opening.

Another misconception is that a two-barrel carburetor will work on a four-barrel manifold (the piece that connects the carburetor to the engine) with the right adapter. This is wrong! An adapter is makeshift at best. Both the carburetor and the manifold should be changed as a set, which is a monstrous job.

A third misconception is that the vacuum and emission-control systems of a vehicle will work properly with any carburetor. They won't—at least not without extensive and knowledgeable reworking. Instead of changing carburetors, buy a dashboard vacuum gauge (see page 82) and train yourself to use it; you'll get the best possible mileage out of your carburetor, no matter how many barrels it has.

A fourth misconception has to do with rebuilt carburetors. If you have your carburetor rebuilt, remind your mechanic to replace the float. (The float "floats" on the gasoline in the fuel bowl to maintain the fuel at the proper

139

level.) There are only a handful of rebuild kits that supply new floats, yet over half of all carburetor failures are caused by defective floats! New floats are sold separately. A carburetor with a bad float can be rebuilt four times, or 400 times, but until the float is replaced, the troubles won't be cured.

While we're on the subject of carburetors, remember there is no such thing as a universal replacement carburetor. There is one manufacturer who sells 1,300 different carburetor models! The sobering thought is that 1,299 of them are the wrong ones for your car. Beware: A new carburetor that actually fits on your car and actually makes it run better than the old one may still be incorrect. Because you can't expect a repair shop to stock all 1,300 carburetors, you will most likely have to special order the right one for your car. You should expect to pay a deposit of at least 50 percent of the retail price. It usually takes one to six weeks for delivery.

Carburetor Fables That Can Cost You

The three carburetor fables that deserve attention center around jets, ice, and floats.

There's a persistent underground folk legend, especially among automotive hobbyists, which says that changing the "jets" in a carburetor will improve performance or increase mileage. Neither is true. Jets are the devices that mix the fuel with air for combustion. They are preset to furnish the engine with the proper fuel to air ratio. Upjetting, which means installing larger jets in order to add more fuel, will not improve power. It distorts the ratio, causes the engine to "run rich," and wastes fuel. Downjetting, installing smaller jets with the intent to economize on fuel, results in too lean a mixture, with insufficient gasoline for the flow of air, which also wastes fuel. Enlarging a jet by drilling is worst of all. A jet has a contour that controls and directs fuel flow into the airstream. Drilling destroys the contour and ruins the jet.

According to another fable, an engine will "breathe better," perform better, and get better mileage if the air-cleaner cover is inverted. There's no truth to this rumor either. Inverting the cover just defeats the air-preheater system, which is there to deliver the right temperature and density of oxygen to your engine.

Not a myth but a common carburetor mystery is "venturi icing." This occurs because every carburetor or fuel injector is like a miniature refrigerator, constantly vaporizing liquid fuel, which cools the venturi or throat of the carburetor. When the temperature and humidity of the outside air are just right, this can cause water vapor to condense and freeze. If this happens, it can cause stalling at idle, rough running at cruising speed, and horrible mileage. It can happen winter or summer, whenever the air temperature is fifty degrees Fahrenheit and above. It almost never happens in extremely cold weather because there's too little water vapor in the air!

Here's how you recognize icing: your engine stalls repeatedly when you take your foot off the gas pedal, but restarts immediately. If this happens on days of high humidity but not on others, you may be experiencing venturi icing. If so, you can add a can of gasoline antifreeze which is water-free alcohol, when you fill your gas tank. The alcohol will reduce the icing and may even eliminate it.

Finally, there's a very specific problem with the carburetors in 1960 to 1981 Chrysler products with slant six-cylinder engines, automatic transmissions, and one-barrel Carter carburetors. The float is mounted in this particular carburetor in such a way that when it gets old and begins to get heavy, it drops a trifle too far. (The float "floats" on the gasoline in the fuel bowl to maintain the proper level.) In a right turn, centrifugal force moves gasoline to the left, raises the float, and the car runs normally. But in a left turn, gasoline crowds to the right, the float drops too far, and the engine tends to flood, often causing the car to stall.

Imagine trying to tell your mechanic that your car stalls whenever you turn left! Who would have known?

The Bad Load of Gas

Every mechanic has heard this story, but it's almost always more imagined than real: "My car was running beautifully until I filled up at a strange station. Fifty miles later it started acting up."

Contaminated gasoline can happen, but it is so rare that most drivers will go through an entire lifetime without the experience. A punctured diaphragm in a vacuum unit, a leak in a PCV hose, or the failure of any of a dozen tuneup parts can all cause sudden rough running, for which "bad gas" gets the blame.

Water in your gas tank *is* bad news, but not, as you would think, because the water gets into your engine. In fact, there have been hundreds of water-injection systems that intentionally introduced water into the intake system of gasoline engines. At the temperatures that exist inside your engine, water instantly becomes steam and passes out the exhaust. What is dangerous about water in your tank is that it can deposit a jellylike "gook" onto the carburetor fuel bowl, jets, and metering rods.

Water in your gas tank is generally not due to a bad load of gas. It usually accumulates one drop at a time. It could be a bit of snow or rain when you're filling up, or overnight condensation. A hundred days, a hundred droplets, and suddenly you have half a cup of water in your tank! Most gasoline blends have an additive to remove the water, but occasionally it's not enough, and you get the gummy buildup.

There are many gasoline driers on the market, and we recommend that you add half a pint of any of these (they all contain anhydrous isopropyl alcohol) to your tank once or twice a year. They are marketed under dozens of brand names that usually include the words "gas drier" or "gas line antifreeze." You can safely buy the least expensive one since they're all the same. Here's how they work: The alcohol seeks out and mixes with any water that's in your tank. This mixture is then flushed out of the gas tank and drawn into your engine. Anything over eighty proof will burn, so a pint of alcohol will eliminate more than a pint of water.

Another way to prevent water problems is to keep your gas tank as full as practical. Driving off the top half of the tank is a good idea anyway. The more gasoline, the less air, so the less water vapor to condense.

Leaded Gasoline Is Better

The reason many people don't like unleaded gasoline is because they think that their engines, especially in older cars, need lead to lubricate the valves. Over the years we've discussed the point with engine designers at two major manufacturers, as well as with a number of engine rebuilders and fleet operators. They are in unanimous agreement: Engines do not, and never did, need lead.

Engines *do* need protection from knock, and for years the only cheap antiknock additives were lead compounds. The antiknock compounds in the earliest lead-free gasolines were not that great, and lead-free gasolines got a bad reputation. Today, new additives make lead-free gasoline better than the best of the old leaded types.

Unleaded gasoline will not damage your valves. It actually keeps your engine cleaner. It will not contaminate your catalytic converter nor poison your lungs. The EPA estimates that 16 percent of gasoline users misfuel their vehicles with leaded gasoline. What many motorists don't realize, however, is that misfueling can cost them an additional nineteen cents per gallon in maintenance costs and decreased performance.

So even though they don't make gasoline like they used to, the news is good. Before the oil embargo of the Seventies, refineries used something called "measured octane" to rate gasoline. Later they began to use a number they called "research octane," which is how a gasoline blend behaves in the laboratory. But the government intervened to try to force the industry back to the original measured octane standards. A compromise resulted. So on today's gas pumps, you'll find an average between research and measured octane. That's why the 87 octane that used to work so well in

"Lead-free gasoline is not new. Over fifty years ago two major refiners marketed unleaded fuel as their "top-of-the-line." T.K.

145

your older car may now make it ping. Switching to premium will solve that problem, but you'll pay 15 to 25 percent more.

With a little experimenting, you can get rid of the ping without spending a lot for gas. Here's how: Have your mechanic retard your timing a degree or two. You may lose 3 percent on your miles per gallon, but you may save 25 percent on the gas you buy and stop the pinging. Another solution is to fill your tank with half premium fuel and half regular. You can experiment with different mixtures to find the cheapest blend that will allow you to drive with only rare pinging.

A note about detergents: You have probably noticed that many of the oil companies are actively promoting detergent gasolines. One reason is because the high repair bills associated with sophisticated fuel-injection systems have been attributed to clogged fuel injectors caused by gasoline. Adding detergent agents to gasoline can reduce clogging and save consumers expensive repair bills.

Today, most auto manufacturers strongly recommend the use of detergent gasolines with their fuel-injected cars. If you need a detergent gasoline, it pays to shop around. Some oil companies offer detergents only in their premium unleaded gasoline, which often costs 15 cents a gallon more than regular. Other oil companies offer detergents in all grades of gasoline. By using a nonpremium grade of detergent gasoline, you can save over $100 per year. Detergent gasolines are *not* necessary for cars with standard carburetors.

The 85 MPG Car

We've all heard rumors about those eighty-five-mile-per-gallon cars that are being kept away from the public. Yes, it's possible to get a reasonably small car to get eighty-five miles per gallon. Here's how: Remove the spare tire, take out the seats, radio, windshield wipers, and battery, get a barefoot, ninety-eight-pound driver, and drive at three miles per hour in idle around a level track—you get the idea.

As competitive as the automobile manufacturing industry is, we're convinced that if an eighty-five-mile-per-gallon car were found today, some car maker would announce marketing plans before noon tomorrow. Nevertheless, every few years there's another round of ads with a lot of fine print telling you how to get the famous 200-mile-per-gallon carburetor that Detroit and the oil companies don't want you to have. When you read the fine print, you find that you're not actually getting a carburetor, but rather a set of plans so you can build your own carburetor, you should know you have tough competition. There are a half dozen major carburetor manufacturers, all with huge research budgets and highly skilled research teams.

Another area of mythology surrounds the much maligned emission-control system. Articles, columns, and letters to the editor still condemn automotive emission controls—usually with the argument that these systems decrease your mileage. Ads in the backs of many hobbyist and do-it-yourself magazines play up this misconception. Some offer to sell "engine breathers" designed to fit all makes and models. The intent of these products is to overcome or bypass a vehicle's emission-control system. This is illegal. In addition, what the seller probably knows, and the purchaser doesn't, is that using one will *damage the engine.*

147

The truth is, a properly maintained emission-control system has an almost undetectable effect on your gas mileage. In fact, while emission standards have grown more stringent, average fuel economy has actually *improved*. Many other examples of quick-fix gadgets and additives can be found in ads in the back of hobby and enthusiast magazines. The ads for the "mileage boosters" are generally the most deceptive. While the words in these ads change over the years, the credo is still *caveat emptor*—buyer beware.

The bottom line is this: Of the hundreds of products on the market that claim to improve your fuel economy, not only do most of them not work, but some may even damage your engine. In addition, you run the risk of voiding your warranty by using these products.

Sometimes the name of the product or promotional material associated with it implies it was endorsed by the federal government. In fact, *no government agency endorses any gas-saving product*. Many of the products, however, have been tested by the Environmental Protection Agency. Of nearly 100 products tested by the EPA, only six have been shown to actually improve your fuel economy. Even these, however, offer such limited savings and are so expensive that we recommend avoiding them.

For a list of gas-saving devices that don't work, you may write to: Merrill Korth, U. S. EPA, 2565 Plymouth Road, Ann Arbor, MI 48105.

If you really want to improve your mileage without damaging your car, see the chapter called *Keeping It Going*.

The Catalytic Converter Test Pipe Scam

There's a gadget called a catalytic converter test pipe that is sold under the legal fiction that a vehicle owner who is not sure if his catalytic converter is working properly, can remove the converter and temporarily replace it with a test pipe—a simple connector without the converter. If his car then runs better, he, theoretically, concludes that his converter is bad and rushes out to buy a new one.

It's not terribly surprising that thousands of these so-called test pipes remain permanently installed. They effectively override the purpose of the catalytic converter and allow polluted air to enter the atmosphere.

A professional mechanic or a muffler shop will usually not install a test pipe. They're illegal if left in place and the professional does not need one to diagnose converter problems. They're also illegal for the do-it-yourselfer to install. Obviously, the FBI is not likely to come and haul you away, but consider this: If you install a test pipe, your car will be contaminating the air the rest of us have to breathe. If that doesn't bother you, your exhaust backpressure will be altered, and the test pipe will cause premature and *expensive* exhaust-valve failure. The laws of emission control are poorly enforced, so you probably won't be arrested. But the laws of physics are perfectly enforced, and they'll get you every time!

Tales of Transmission Fluid and Timing Belts

There is another myth that suggests you put a half pint of automatic-transmission fluid in your engine oil and another in your gas tank in order to reverse engine wear.

Automatic-transmission fluid is great stuff—for your automatic transmission. Put it in your engine oil, and it will reduce viscosity and contribute to premature wear. Put it in your gasoline, and it will reduce volatility and cause hard starts and poor mileage. No matter what story you've heard, your car runs on principles of physics, not magic.

The timing belt is what keeps your spark plugs in time with your engine. One myth suggests that you should replace the belt before you have a breakdown. Dealers, on the other hand, claim that they'll last up to 60,000 miles. Which is true?

Newer timing belts are made of neoprene, which is both pliable and durable. They cost only a few dollars, but the labor to replace them is considerable. In the interest of fiscal sanity, we usually suggest that unless something is broken, don't fix it. So don't replace a perfectly good belt that may run for another four years. Timing belts are engineered to last from 80,000 to 100,000 miles. Your car will be disabled only if the belt breaks or is so badly worn that the teeth skip a notch or two on a gear. Long before this happens, there will be visible signs of wear, which will produce erratic engine performance.

Beginning at 60,000 miles, we suggest inspecting the belt carefully at every tuneup. If cracks are discernible, or if the edges of the teeth or ridges are worn and rounded, replace the belt. If it passes the visual inspection, keep it for another year.

Slow Down: With Brakes or Engine?

As anyone with a manual transmission knows, to slow down you have your choice of downshifting or braking. However, you may have been told that downshifting is bad for the transmission and that it's cheaper to repair brakes than transmissions or engines. This old myth has always been wrong.

First of all, brakes fade; engine compression does not. Therefore, in stop-and-go driving, excessive use of the brakes can cause them to overheat, fade, or fail when you need them most. Second, professionals agree that downshifting causes no more wear than allowing the engine to run at idle. On the other hand, overusing your brakes will definitely cause them to wear faster. Finally, and this is especially true in traffic, shifting down keeps the engine speed and driveshaft (or wheel speed), in the proper relationship to each other. If traffic opens up and you can accelerate, you are already in the proper gear to do so if you've downshifted. Not only is this faster and safer, but it's easier on the transmission and engine, because it avoids "lugging" the engine. Lugging occurs when you try to accelerate from too low a speed in too high a gear and can cause serious engine damage.

Shifting down was right when you learned to drive, and it still is. Just don't ride the clutch!

YOU CAN DO IT YOURSELF!

During the past few years thousands of service stations have disappeared and the number of cars and trucks on the road has increased. Combine this with the fact that the average age of cars on the road is now over seven years and what do you have? More cars, needing more service, with fewer places to fix them. There are two obvious results: Crowded repair shops and an increase in the number of people willing to try a few repairs themselves.

To keep your car in top shape, it will need maintenance. On newer, more computerized cars some maintenance tasks are simply not recommended for the average person. However, there are still many things you can do yourself. Not only will that save you money, but you will gain a better understanding of how your car works, which will pay off in getting those repairs done correctly that you can't do yourself.

How much you will save by doing a job yourself is based on how much a repair shop would charge for the labor to do the job. Let's consider the task of changing the oil and filter. The most popular "flat rate" book says this would take a typical mechanic two-tenths of an hour to change the oil and another two-tenths to change the filter. At a shop rate of forty dollars per hour, that adds up to sixteen dollars. In addition, you'll pay full list price for both the oil and the filter. So, changing your own oil and filter will save you about twenty dollars.

Replacing an alternator can easily save you twenty dollars in labor charges and you'll scarcely get your fingertips dirty. Renewing a starter, candidly a messy job, can easily save from twenty-eight dollars to thirty-six dollars, depending on the make and model.

If you ever want to know the labor charge for a specific job, ask your mechanic if you can look it up in his flat rate book. Most mechanics will be happy to give you this kind of information and offer advice on do-it-yourself work. This is partly because most good shops have enough business and most mechanics want to keep your good will for other jobs. Be careful not to mislead him by asking for an estimate; that would be an unfair use of his time and office supplies. Let him know you're merely asking for the amount of *time* assigned for the job in his flat rate manual. Then multiply that by his shop rate per hour to arrive at a rough idea of how much doing the job yourself will save you.

Doing the job right can depend on the reliability of the parts you buy. It's frustrating to do work that you expected to last for 12,000 miles, then find you must do the job over after 3,000 or 4,000 miles because the "bargain" parts you bought begin to fail. As a do-it-yourselfer, you're already saving on labor, and you can invest part of your savings in excellent parts, especially since they cost less per mile.

A genuine cost factor for do-it-yourselfers is determining correct service intervals. Low-mileage, late model automobiles have been reduced to virtually worthless hulks because the owners neglected routine maintenance, such as changing the engine oil and the filter. Other owners have wasted money tuning up their cars more frequently than needed. The key is to find the sensible middle ground. The owner's manual will have suggestions and so will parts manufacturers. However these sources have some built-in bias. Part of the job of the owner's manual's is to convince you what a great car you bought, often by suggesting service intervals longer than good sense would dictate. Part of the job of the parts manufacturers' ads is to sell you the manufacturers' products, sometimes more frequently than you truly need them. Therefore, the best source of information about your car and its service requirements is a trusted mechanic at a reliable shop.

We have organized this chapter beginning with some of the easiest do-it-yourself items and progressing to some of the more time-consuming. Notice we didn't say difficult. All of these repairs and checks could be accomplished by a novice. You'll find that your confidence will improve the more you do. Even if you decide that doing it yourself is not for you, reading through these items will help you understand what you are paying for and put you in the position of getting the right job done right!

When you set out to do-it-yourself, you can do the job right, or you can do the job over.

One of the most frustrating experiences for any do-it-yourselfer is deciding if a part is defective. Without test equipment, most do-it-yourselfers troubleshoot by substitution—replacing the suspected problem part with a brand new one, only to discover that the original symptoms persist. One way to avoid this problem is to have a mechanic test and diagnose the problem and test your work when you are finished. You'll have to pay for the tests, but you save by doing the right job.

"A new customer came into my shop in a late-model pickup. The engine was running rough, backfiring, overheating, and gas mileage was poor.

One of his friends assured him his trouble was caused by his carburetor, so he bought a new, top-of-the-line replacement for about $175. The problems persisted. Another friend suggested the problem was with the ignition coil, so he installed a heavy-duty racing model. A brother-in-law suspected the distributor, so the owner installed a high-performance, dual-point distributor. Spark plugs were replaced twice and new "high performance" plug wires, an electric fuel pump, PCV valve, and air filter were installed. After over $500, the original problems were unchanged!

I hooked up the engine to the scope and analyzer, and found the trouble in about two minutes. There was a severe vacuum leak at the intake manifold gasket, about a ten dollar part. If my customer had let me test first, he'd have been $500 ahead.

The point is that you should never troubleshoot by substitution. Pay your mechanic for a test, and then you'll be sure that your efforts will pay off." T.K.

Getting Help

As surprising as it may seem, one of the best sources of do-it-yourself advice is your regular mechanic. Professionals will often help do-it-yourselfers for a number of reasons. Many mechanics began as do-it-yourselfers and feel an identification with the struggling beginner. Most good professional mechanics have all the work they want to handle and don't mind encouraging do-it-yourselfers. All mechanics realize the do-it-yourself movement is not going to go away, and that it's smart business to give good advice which gains customer good will and attracts people back to the shop for work that must be done professionally.

Getting free advice from a mechanic involves some common sense. You'll encounter more cooperation on a rainy Tuesday when the shop is not swamped with deadlines than on a frantic Saturday morning. If you need your mechanic's attention for a long period, say twenty minutes or more, and if your car is with you, offer to pay him for his time, and don't be too surprised if he charges you. That's only fair, since his time and skill are what he sells.

In addition to your mechanic, there are at least three major publishers of general repair manuals. Two of these manuals, *Motor* and *Mitchell's,* are distributed directly from a publisher's representative to mechanics and repair shops. That doesn't mean you can't buy one, they're just a little harder to find. Ask your regular mechanic for the addresses and phone numbers of the sales representatives. The third major repair manual, *Chilton's,* is marketed through parts stores and regular bookstores.

All the manuals are divided into separate volumes for domestic and imported cars, and are published by model year. A given volume will go back five to seven years from its cover date, so if you have a six or seven year old car,

"Do-it-yourselfers should work with their regular mechanic as partners. You can install the new parts, then have him scope, analyze, and adjust. His experience assures that you've done your work right and haven't overlooked anything." T.K.

you'll want to be sure the book you buy goes back that far. All the books feature excellent photographs and drawings, with well-written, understandable text. These manuals apply to a single car: one make, one model year. Even if you are not much of a do-it-yourselfer, consider investing in one. If it goes out of print it could be a valuable asset when you sell your car.

Let's make the distinction between the owner's manual and the shop manual. The owner's manual is furnished at no extra cost with every new car. It explains how to operate the windshield washer or to release the parking brake. It may also remind you that drive belt tension should be set every six months and that your turn signals require a number 1157 lamp. But it will not tell you how to adjust the brake or how to get at bulbs to change them. That information comes from the shop manual.

The shop manual will guide you, step by step, with clear photographs and precise text, through the rebuilding of your automatic transmission, if that's your wish. It will also provide equally clear instructions for removing the tail light cover to replace a burned-out bulb. Tuneup instructions, timing procedures, brake information, and much more are included in the shop manual.

Safety and Tool Tips

Working on a car doesn't have to be hazardous, but there is always the potential for serious injury. The way to prevent injury is to recognize the dangers and use the same procedures the pros use to avoid them. First and most important, never rush your work. Instead, plan your work deliberately and anticipate the result of each action. If you're tackling an unfamiliar job, talk it over with your regular mechanic. Here are some things to keep in mind when tackling a repair job:

- Always use the correct tool for the job.
- Use a tool tray and put tools away, clean, the moment you're finished with them. Slipping on a forgotten tool can result in serious injury.
- All power tools should be grounded or double insulated.
- Have plenty of light.
- Protect your eyes from the following hazards: battery acid, sharp metal particles, flying springs, tools with pointed edges, dirt, and abrasives. Regular eye glasses provide almost no protection. You need OSHA-approved safety goggles as a minimum. They're not expensive, and they can be worn over eyeglasses.

Tool Tips

The right tool can make a difficult job easy and the wrong one can make an easy job hard. This section provides some general advice on tools that will come in handy for repair jobs. How many tools you have is a function of how much you feel comfortable doing.

For basic pliers we suggest the adjustable joint variety. Noticeably longer than common pliers, they have jaws that are tilted about thirty degrees away from the handles and a long groove on one side which allows them to be adjusted from a small to a large opening.

Because of their design, adjustable joint pliers allow enormous amounts of leverage on a great variety of work, without marring the surface of the work.

Another pair of pliers worth owning are snipe-nose pliers. These look like ordinary needle nose pliers, except that they are drastically slimmed down toward the tip. Because they are both strong and slender, snipe-nose pliers are difficult and expensive to manufacture. Snipe nose pliers have a number of uses including positioning tiny parts and pulling broken keys out of locks.

Your tool box should also contain some clamping pliers and an adjustable wrench. The clamping pliers have jaws that wrap around objects and seize them in an adjustable vise grip. The adjustable wrench has two crescent- shaped jaws, one of which is slid along the other by an adjustable knob.

Another useful tool for do-it-yourselfers is a screw starter. You'll really appreciate one if you've ever had to install a small screw in a difficult-to-reach place. A screw starter costs only a few dollars. You will probably want one for straight screws and for Phillips head screws.

Something you will find on newer cars is a Torx head screw. The shape of the head is patented and it requires a patented screw driver. Car makers are using these screws on headlights, lens covers, dashboards, interior trim of all kinds, and parts of the engine. You will need a Torx head screwdriver to work with these screws. There is a different driver for each size and each grips and holds the screw in any position, including straight down, and won't let go until you want it to.

If you get serious about do-it-yourself work, consider buying a volt-ohm-milliammeter, or multi-meter. It can help you solve dozens of problems around your car, from checking the resistance of spark plug wires to testing light bulbs.

Don't be put off because a multi-meter looks complicated at first glance. The dashboard of your car would be bewildering to a person who had never seen one. You can learn to use the instrument one function at a time. If you buy a good meter, it will come with a complete instruction book.

Buying Parts

There are three basic options for repair parts: new, remanufactured, and used parts.

New parts are available from car dealers and auto parts stores, remanufactured parts are usually available at auto parts stores only and used parts are found at wrecking yards.

To make a decision between new or remanufactured parts for your car, consider the difference in price, the identity and reputation of the remanufacturer, and the kind of warranty you get. Remanufactured parts will cost at least 25 percent less than new ones.

In some cases, the remanufacturers are the same companies as the original equipment manufacturers, rebuilding their own components. Most of the time, though, they are smaller, local companies that specialize in a few kinds of parts.

Auto parts remanufacturing should not be confused with the sometimes shoddy "rebuilding" of the part. A remanufactured alternator, for example, only uses the old case, armature shaft, and winding frames. The old copper windings are removed and new wire, new bearings, new diodes, and new terminals, are installed. The finished product is bench tested before being packed. It is the mechanical and electrical equivalent of a new alternator, and carries the same warranty.

There are two basic types of parts stores, wholesale and retail. Retail parts stores are either local or part of a national chain. The national chain variety look like a modern hardware or department store. The local stores will resemble an old fashioned hardware store. A typical retail parts store will stock over 100,000 parts. Wholesale stores, which are often open to the public, can stock as many as one million parts. At a wholesale store, you usually place an order for a part at a desk.

The clerks have access to huge catalogues which will help them find just the right part for your car. Individuals who buy parts at wholesale stores usually pay retail prices. When mechanics go in, they usually pay wholesale prices.

Used parts are generally purchased at a wrecking yard. Most of us want to save money any way we can, and many wrecked cars have perfectly good parts at substantial savings. On large parts, such as engines or transmissions, a wrecking yard can save you 50 percent of the cost of a new unit. When buying a used part, carefully check out your guarantee and return privileges in case the part doesn't work or doesn't fit.

We offer this advice in deciding what parts to buy: For parts that wear out periodically, such as wiper blades, spark plugs, ignition points, and other low cost items, always buy new. Parts such as wheel covers, bumpers, body sections, and trim are perfectly acceptable used.

Pre-Trip Inspection and Winterizing

This is one of the easiest and most important jobs you can do. The job will go faster if you have someone to help you by operating switches and controls.

First, check your engine oil. Top it off if necessary, but don't overfill. Check your coolant level, and fill radiator or reservoir with a fifty-fifty mixture of water and coolant. Top off your windshield washer fluid. Inspect the water level in your battery. Use distilled water if you need to add some. Check your tires and make sure they have at least a quarter-inch of tread depth before a long trip. A tire with one-sixteenth or less is not only unsafe, it's illegal. Check the power steering fluid if your car has power steering.

Next, test all the lights. Have your helper turn on high and low beam headlights, parking lights, turn signals, emergency flasher, brake lights, and backup lights. To test the lights, you'll need to have the ignition switch on. Replace all burned-out bulbs. Test your horn and windshield wipers and replace worn blade inserts. After a five-minute minimum warmup, check the automatic transmission fluid level. Add some of the proper type if necessary.

On your trip carry spare oil and water, a flashlight, safety flares, tools, and some duct tape.

Winterizing Your Car

There's more to "winterizing" your car than checking your antifreeze. However, that's the best place to start. Your parts store can sell you an inexpensive coolant tester which will tell you the freeze protection of the mixture in your radiator. But if the mixture is rusty looking or if it's been in the car for two years or more, you should drain, flush, and refill with a fresh fifty-fifty mixture of water and coolant.

Autumn is a good time to think about new tire chains. If yours are worn or if you don't own them, you will want to buy the right type for your tires. On the first snowy day, there will be long lines, short supplies, and no bargains.

Don't overlook your windshield washer. On freezing glass, plain water will turn to ice, and if the weather is cold enough, the mechanism may freeze and break. Your parts store will sell you a number of products that will help melt ice and snow on the windshield and that will also protect the washer mechanism.

Give your battery and charging system some careful scrutiny. Have your mechanic test the battery, alternator, and regulator. It's an inexpensive and quick job.

A little time spent in advance on each of these items will help you drive through winter in comfort and safety—and you can do most of them yourself.

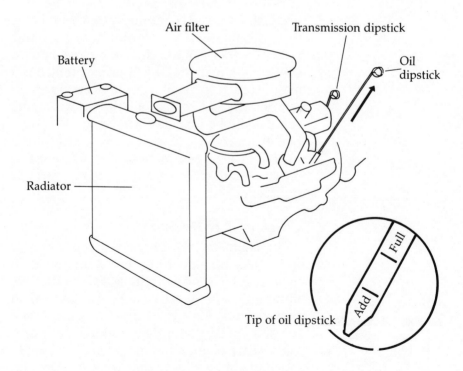

Checking Your Oil and Transmission Fluid

Replacing Wiper Inserts and Checking Tire Pressure

Changing wiper inserts is one of the easiest do-it-yourself projects, but be sure you know which parts to buy. Asking for the wrong part can cost you! It's reasonable to assume that when your windshield wipers start to streak you need new wiper blades. But that's wrong! "Blade" is the name the parts industry gives to the entire assembly attached to the wiper arm. It consists of the springy metal support with its elaborate hinging and clamps, plus the black neoprene strip, which is called a wiper blade *insert* or *refill*. It's the insert that wears out, not the whole blade. Whether you do it yourself or have someone else do it, ask for new wiper blade inserts or refills, not wiper blades. Blades can cost ten times as much as inserts.

To install the new inserts all you need to understand is the clamping system that holds it in the blade. If you're not sure how this system works, ask the clerk at a parts store to show you when you buy your new refills. You may need a pair of needle-nose pliers to remove the old refills, but the replacements can usually be installed with finger pressure. Blade inserts are marketed in lengths from twelve to eighteen inches, so you'll want to measure your old ones to be sure you buy the right length.

Checking Tire Pressure

An estimated 60 percent of automobiles have tires inflated to incorrect pressure. In most cases, because of tiny leaks, the tires are underinflated and are wearing out faster than they should. Also, the rolling resistance of a too-soft tire is greater than it should be, meaning you are using more fuel than is needed to move the car. Finally, if one front tire is significantly softer than the other, the result is a

"When buying new wiper blade inserts, bring your old ones along to make sure you're getting just the right part." J.G.

steering pull in the direction of the underinflated tire. This produces a slight, but measurable amount of unnecessary wear on front suspension components.

Tire overinflation is also bad, causing more premature wear than does underinflation. An overinflated tire will cause steering pull in the direction of a properly-inflated tire.

The simple solution is to check your tire pressure once a month. In order to do this you will need a tire gauge. The most common one is the size of a pencil and slips over the tire valve. The reason you need a gauge is because service station air pumps are notoriously inaccurate.

One of the best rated and least expensive gauges is available from the Tire Industry Safety Council. Send $2 to the Council, Box 1801, Dept. AM, Washington, D.C. 20013 and ask for their tire gauge and information booklet.

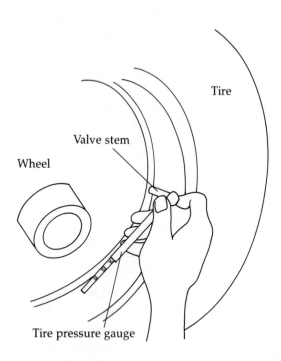

Checking Your Tire Pressure

Caring for Vinyl

Some parts of your car are likely to be made of vinyl. Typically, vinyl is used on rooftops and trim outside the car, plus the dash, door panels, and upholstery inside the car. Vinyl's enemies are dirt, temperature changes, and ultraviolet light. When vinyl begins to dry out and become brittle, tiny cracks begin to appear in the surface.

Fortunately, maintenance is easy. A soft, damp cloth will remove dust and most dirt, and there are a number of excellent vinyl dressing products on the market. A good vinyl dressing replaces missing oils to the material to restore softness and resiliency. It also flushes out deeply embedded dust and, as it dries, it fills the tiny cracks. Finally, it acts as a sealer, to keep dust particles out, and to minimize the effects of ultraviolet light.

Vinyl dressing also restores the appearance of the material. The use of vinyl dressing is one of the most simple and cost effective maintenance jobs anyone can do.

If you rip or puncture something made of vinyl, there is a new vinyl repair kit that is very easy to use. A cut or ripped seam in vinyl auto upholstery used to be a tragedy. Fabric upholstery was comparatively easy to handle, and one could manage a reasonable looking repair. But vinyl upholstery doesn't take kindly to punctures by needles. Any attempt to sew it usually results in a mess. To the rescue comes a vinyl repair kit that uses a bead of transparent adhesive to make rips literally disappear. It takes twenty-four hours to set and can be used on punctures, straight cuts, and even V-shaped rips. You simply surround the damaged area with masking tape, leaving a quarter of an inch of vinyl around the problem exposed. Finally, simply squeeze on the vinyl repair material. Some cuts may require two applications.

Changing Light Bulbs

The biggest problem with changing bulbs is sometimes just getting at them. To replace a burned-out bulb, you may need a Phillips or Torx screwdriver. Some bulbs are changed from inside the trunk or engine compartment, others by removing the lens cover. Check the shop manual for the appropriate method for your car or ask a friendly mechanic. At the parts store you must provide the year, make, and model of your car and function of each bulb you need. If possible, bring the old bulb for exact identification.

One light that you will become very dependent on is the courtesy light that turns on when a door opens. This is a relatively simple bulb to replace. If you see two or three screws holding the cover, take them out carefully so as not to lose them. Most plastic covers are a squeeze fit, and must be squeezed to be removed. Do so gently as they are breakable. Use a rag to remove the burned-out bulb. A word of caution: When you install the new bulb, be sure the car door is closed. That new bulb is brighter than you think and it gets hot quickly.

Your headlights can be surprisingly difficult to change. Some have clamps that are spring loaded and snap off, others may be attached with fiendishly concealed screws which require patented Torx drivers to remove and others release from inside the hood. Guess wrong and a simple job can take half a day or, worse yet, result in a botched job and expensive damage. Before changing your headlights make sure you know the procedure, and be very careful not to disturb the two aiming screws. They are right next to three mounting screws you must loosen, but look different. An illustrated shop manual could pay for itself on this job alone.

"A headlight may cost between five and ten dollars, but by putting it in yourself you should save a fifteen dollar installation charge." J.G.

Opening a Frozen Car Lock

When the weather dips below freezing, especially if there's been a snowfall or freezing rain, a large number of drivers discover they can't unlock their car door, due to a frozen lock. If you're faced with the problem of a frozen door lock, first try all the other doors on the car. Often the wind direction or exposure of the car will be such that only one side is actually frozen. If that trick doesn't work, a hair dryer works beautifully if you're within an extension cord's reach of electricity. Another trick is to heat up the key in the flame of a match or cigarette lighter and repeatedly insert it into the lock. All you need do is get the temperature of the lock above the freezing point.

Once you have it open, remember, it will freeze again! It's not the lock that freezes, it's water. Moisture may have run into or condensed inside the lock cylinder. To prevent the problem again, shoot a short burst of spray from a pressurized can of penetrating oil. This will displace any moisture present, lubricate the lock, and prevent it from freezing on the next cold morning. There are also special lock lubricants at your parts store which contain penetrating oil and powdered graphite.

Changing a Tire

Knowing how to change a tire can save you as much as fifty dollars in tow truck fees *and* get you back on the road faster. Your owner's manual contains instructions on finding the tire-changing equipment and where to position your jack.

You may want to buy and keep in your trunk one of the good quality X-shaped lug wrenches the pros use when they don't have an air ratchet handy. It is much easier to use than the wrenches that come with most cars. It's also a good idea to carry an old towel or blanket to kneel on.

Park on a level spot as far from traffic as possible and take the spare out of the trunk before you begin work. Make sure the spare is inflated. Remove the wheel cover and slightly loosen the lug nuts *before* you jack the car off the ground. Sometimes it can require a mighty tug. Using rocks or chunks of wood, block the front and back of the wheel diagonally opposite the one you're changing. Set the parking brake and leave the transmission in gear, or in *park* if it's an automatic. Jack the car high enough so the inflated spare will fit. While the car is on the jack, don't ever get in a position where the car may fall on you.

You should *never* use a bumper jack to hold up the car if you need to get underneath it. Bumper jacks can slip and cause very serious injuries. If you must work under a car, only use the bumper jack to lift the car high enough to slip two concrete blocks or pieces of timber under two wheels. Then carefully block the wheels still on the ground, so the car can't roll off. Another idea is to park your car with one or two wheels on a tall curb, or position it over a gully. That way, all four wheels are on the ground and you have enough room to work underneath in complete safety.

Changing Your Air Filter

One of the easiest filters to change is your air filter. You usually can tell that the filter needs changing by looking at it. Hold the filter up to a light; if you can't see light through it, change it. Another test is to try the following: When your engine has warmed up, put the car in *park* or *neutral,* and with the emergency brake on, let the car idle. Open the filter lid and remove the filter. If the engine begins to run faster, you need to change the filter.

Make sure you purchase the exact replacement filter. Like most parts, air filters are sold by a part number. An underhood decal will often tell you your air filter number and your owner's manual may be helpful. An auto parts store will know if you give them the year, make, model, and engine size of your car. Also find out if your car has a "breather" filter. It's two to four inches long, about a half-inch thick, and it fits in a pocket inside the air cleaner housing. Also available at a parts store, it should be replaced each time the air filter is changed.

Once you have the new filter, raise the hood and remove the cover of the air cleaner. On many cars this requires loosening a single wing nut, bolts or clamps. In a few cases, air or vacuum hoses may be in the way. If you can lift out the cover and filter without disturbing the hoses, do so. If hoses must be disconnected to make room, *label them first.* Masking tape and a felt pen work well. Don't be concerned with the name or function of each hose, just make sure you put hose *A* back on fitting *A* and hose *B* on fitting *B*.

With the old filter removed, use a soft rag or paper towels to wipe clean the inside of the air cleaner and its cover. Put in the new filter (and breather filter) and replace the cover.

Replacing Your Car's Battery

When you buy a new battery make sure it's fresh and fully charged. Look for a battery with easily removable filler caps so you can check water level and add distilled water as needed. Before beginning, remember an automobile battery is heavy. There's strong sulfuric acid in the battery, so you'll want to wear old clothing.

First, remove the cables starting with the negative (-) terminal. Then unclamp the battery and take it out. Be careful—it's heavy. Next, thoroughly clean the supporting tray and inspect the old cable clamps. If they're worn or corroded, or if they won't clean up with a wire brush, replace them. Your parts store will sell you new clamps of either type, side mount or top mount. If you need only new bolts, your parts store sells those individually.

Put the new battery in position, clamp it down and reconnect the cables. Check to make sure the positive cable is connected to the positive (+) terminal and the negative to the negative (-). Then check it again. And recheck. A good way to ruin a new battery is to hook it up backwards. Use wrenches, not pliers, to tighten the clamp bolts.

Before you buy a new battery, you should check to see if your old one may just need to be cleaned. For example, if your car is exhibiting symptoms such as dim headlights, hard starts, a weak horn, and generally poor battery performance, the cure is usually cleaning it up.

To clean a battery, first remove the cables. Remember to disconnect the negative terminal first and to reconnect it last. Always use the proper size wrench and *never* use pliers or vise grips. If the bolts are badly corroded, your parts store can sell you specially coated new ones. Next, clean off the oily film that forms on the battery with a soft rag. If there is visible

"Don't believe the old fable that if you set a battery down on concrete, the concrete somehow "drains" the power out of the battery and ruins it. The tale originated because many garages have concrete floors and garages often keep batteries sitting around for long periods of time. Sitting around, these batteries lose their charge, become sulfated and are ruined. Because most garage floors are concrete, it was assumed that the concrete was causing the problem. They could have been set on wood, rubber, or steel and would still be ruined, simply because they sat around." T.K.

corrosion at either terminal, clean it off with a little warm water and dishwashing liquid. Use a *nonmetallic* brush, to avoid causing a short circuit. Then rinse the battery with clean water and use some sandpaper or steel wool to shine the terminal posts and cable ends.

No matter what you may have heard or read elsewhere *never use baking soda to clean your battery!* There is strong sulfuric acid in your battery. Baking soda is sodium bicarbonate, an alkali. If enough baking soda splashed or leaked into the battery through a crack, it could cause damage to the battery and an explosion that could seriously injure you.

When everything is clean and dry and put back together, coat the terminals with a heavy layer of common petroleum jelly and they'll stay that way for a long time.

Use a plastic or wood-and-bristle brush to clean battery terminals or the surface of the battery itself while everything is hooked up. A metal brush is a conductor, and can cause a shower of sparks and a surprising amount of heat if it completes a path from positive terminal to ground, while both terminals are connected.

Check the battery fluid level once a month and more often in warm weather. If you allow the fluid level to drop, you can void the warranty on your new battery. If the level is low, do not use plain tap water to top it off. Tap water contains minerals which can contaminate the battery and shorten its life. Add distilled water from the supermarket or hardware store.

With proper maintenance a battery can last the life of the car.

Changing the Engine Oil

One of the first tasks many do-it-yourselfers perform is changing the engine oil.

You'll need just a few tools. First, is a wrench to fit the drain plug, a filter wrench to remove the old filter, a drain pan to catch the oil, an old plastic jug, and a large funnel. You'll also need oil and a new filter. Check your owner's manual for the right type of oil (and amount) and filter. We suggest buying oil in the one-quart plastic containers which are easy to handle.

Wear old clothes. A cap and gloves are optional items to keep your hair and hands clean. Dirty oil can leave stains on your skin. There are hand-protecting creams on the market that are resistant to oil and wash off easily with soap and water.

Park the car in a safe, level spot, position the drain pan under the oil pan and remove the oil drain plug. You may have to hunt around for it the first time. It will be at a low point under the engine. After the oil stops dripping, *replace the plug.* Then re-position the pan and remove the old oil filter, using your new filter wrench. Be careful, the filter holds up to a quart of dirty oil.

Install the new filter, following the directions on its package, which will include running your oil-soaked fingertip around the new gasket, and installing the filter by hand, without a wrench. Double-check that you have replaced the plug and put in all but a quart of the new oil. Run the engine for two minutes to pump air out and oil into the new filter, then check the dipstick and top off to the proper level.

To dispose of the used oil, use the funnel to pour it into the plastic jug. Most service stations will accept your old oil, though some may charge a small fee.

"After you clean up, take your car in for a chassis lubrication. It's good to get in the habit of getting a lube job whenever you change the oil."
J.G.

173

INDEX

A

advertised specials, *123*
air filter, *56, 170*
air conditioner, *87*
air injector reactor, *67*
alternator light, *107*
American Petroleum Institute
 (API), *76*
amps, *107*
antifreeze, *78, 143*
automatic transmission fluid
 (ATF), *77*
Automotive Service Excellence
 (ASE), *15*
average driving conditions, *135*

B

backfiring, *58, 106*
baking soda, *88, 172*
battery, *88, 104, 171*
battery fluid, *172*
belts, *86*
Better Business Bureau, *45*
brake failure, *115*
brake fluid, *65, 86*
brake warning light, *115*
brakes, *64, 86, 93, 114, 151*

C

carbon dioxide, *67*
carbon monoxide, *67*
carburetor, *57, 109, 139, 141*
catalytic converter, *66, 149*
Chilton's, 156
choke vacuum pulloff, *103*

choke, *63*
comeback customer, *23, 37*
complaints, *40*
compression ratio, *53*
coolant, *79, 103, 112*
coolant recovery tank, *112*
counterfeit parts, *128*
credit card, *136*
cylinder firing order, *58*

D

deceleration valve, *106*
detailing, *93*
diesel engine, *21, 55*
dimmer switch, *117*
distributor, *60*
drive train, *93*
driving habits, *91*
duct tape, *96*

E

electric fan, *113*
emission control system
 (ECS), *66*
engine, *21, 51, 54, 78, 103, 112,
 117*
engine overheating, *51, 103, 112*
Environmental Protection
 Agency, *145, 148*
ethylene glycol, *78*
exhaust manifold, *68*
exhaust gas recirculation (ERG)
 valve, *53, 138*
exhaust system, *117*

F

Fair Credit Reporting Act, *134*
fans, *113*
Federal Trade Commission, *133*
fire, *118*
firing order, *58,*
flat rate book, *124*
float, *57, 139, 142*
frozen door lock, *168*
fuel filter, *69*
fuel-air mixture, *56, 61, 117*

G

gasoline, *80, 85, 145*
gasoline drier, *143*
gasoline leaks, *116*

H

headlights, *117*
horsepower, *52*
hoses, *93*
hydrocarbons, *67*

I

ignition 60, *137*
internal vacuum- sensing
   diaphragm, *106*

J

jets, *141*
jump start, *89*

K

knocks (engine), *83*

L

light bulbs, *167*
Lincoln penny test, *90*

M

mechanic certification, *15*
metallic sounds, *114*
methanol, *85*
middle-aged car care, *93*
mileage, *126*

miles per gallon (MPG), *82*
Mitchell's, 156
Motor, 156

N

National Automobile Dealers
   Association, *45*

O

octane, *83, 145*
oil, *75, 173*
oil dipstick, *163*
oil filter, *75*
original equipment
   manufacturer (OEM), *128*
oscilloscope, *137*
owner's manual, *157*

P

PCV hose, *109, 143*
pliers, *159*
pollution, *67*
positive crankcase ventilation
(PCV) valve, *66*
power brakes, *64*
power steering, *64*
pre-trip inspection, *162*
preservice interview, *29*
preventive maintenance, *73, 92*

R

remanufacturers, *160*
remanufactured parts, *160*
repair shop, *13, 130*
repair parts, *34, 160*
repairs, *22*

S

S-T-O-P: A-OK, 107
safety, *158*
self-service stations, *75*
service grades, *76*
shifting down, *151*
shock absorbers, *129*
shop manual, *157*
skid marks, *110*
Society of Automotive
   Engineers, *52*

spark plug, *58, 60,137*
spark plug wires, *58 , 88, 125,126*
stalling, *85, 106*
starting problems, *103*
steering wheel vibration, *110*
steering, *86*
steering wheel, *119*

T

temperature, *107*
test pipe, *67, 149*
thermostat, *51*
Tire Industry Safety Council,
   119, 165
tire gauge, *119, 165*
tire changing, *169*
tire pressure, *119, 164*
tires, *90, 93*
tire chains, *95*
tools, *36, 95, 158*
Torx head screwdriver, *159*
transmission fluid, *62, 77, 150*
transmission (automatic), *62, 77*
tuneup, *137, 150*
turbocharger, *56*

U

undriven car, *97*
upholstery (vinyl), *166*
used car dealers, *93*
used parts, *161*

V

V belt, 59, 64
vacuum gauge, *82*
vacuum leak, *106*
venturi icing, *141*
vinyl, *166*
viscosity, *75, 150*
volt-ohm- milliammeter
   (VOM), *159*

W

warranties, *42, 127*
wax, *98*
wheel bearings, *110*
wheel balancing, *71*
winterizing, *162*
wiper blade inserts, *164*